by the same author

The Big Easy *(a novel)*

Judge

The
Life
and
Times
of
Leander
Perez

Judge

The Life and Times of Leander Perez

James Conaway

Alfred A. Knopf
New York
1973

THIS IS A BORZOI BOOK
PUBLISHED BY ALFRED A. KNOPF, INC.

Library of Congress Cataloging in Publication Data

Conaway, James.   Judge: the life and times of
Leander Perez.

1. Perez, Leander Henry, 1891–1969.
I. Title.
KF373.P47C65   345'.73'0750924   [B]   73-7267
ISBN 0-394-47429-5

Manufactured in the United States of America
First Edition

For my parents

The most dangerous form of pride is neither arrogance nor humility, but its mild, common denominator form, complacency.

James Agee,
Let Us Now Praise Famous Men

Contents

Judge

The
Life
and
Times
of
Leander
Perez

Chapter One

Up from Bottom

Always take the offensive. The defensive ain't worth a damn.

> *Leander Perez*

Man . . .

The free ferry at Pointe a la Hache, Plaquemines Parish, Louisiana, carries travelers between the east and west banks of the Mississippi River with absolute regularity. A plaque displayed on the wheelhouse states that the ferry was built without bond issue or taxation by the Plaquemines Parish (county) Commission Council, and bears the name JUDGE L. H. PEREZ, PRESIDENT in letters as large as those designating the ferry's berth.

The arch over the entrance to reclaimed Fort Jackson, just south on Highway 23, also bears a plaque on which a Rebel and an American flag are crossed, and it praises Perez for "his efforts to preserve our liberties, freedoms and way of life." Another plaque reads, "The bricks forming this arch were bought individually by the people of Plaquemines Parish and it was erected by them as a lasting token of their esteem and admiration for Judge L. H. Perez."

Plaquemines's congressman, F. Edward Hébert, and several Louisiana state legislators favor a plan for constructing a statue of Perez to be made of pennies collected from schoolchildren throughout the South. The pennies would be melted down and cast into a likeness of Perez in some characteristic pose; the statue might then be placed atop the one-hundred-foot smokestack of a deserted paper mill, facing south toward

4

ships plowing up the river from the Gulf of Mexico, and be-
yond.

Leander Henry Perez was a master politician and an exceptional constitutional lawyer, a social reformer, and an out-
wardly religious man devoted to his family; he was also obsessed with power, ruthless, fraudulent, and sentimental, and a
bigot. He created, ruled, and perpetuated one of the most
formidable political machines in America, lubricated by money
from the vast mineral deposits in Plaquemines and sanctified
by a new parish charter which he himself devised. Perez died
in March 1969, but his two sons rule on. Plaquemines today
is an oligarchy which seems determined to transform itself into
America's only constitutional monarchy.

Perez remained in power for almost half a century, from
the end of World War I through the Great Society. He was
partly responsible for preventing the impeachment of Huey
Long; he went on to become a powerful and reactionary force
in Louisiana and the South as a whole, organizing an extensive
network of segregationist and states' rights organizations, defy-
ing federal courts and the Catholic Church, and at home becoming the embodiment of the law in an area that is naturally
isolated. In some ways Plaquemines could be seen as a compo-
site of an earlier America—rich in natural resources, populated by a diverse people who were unsophisticated, tenacious,
and basically decent; in Plaquemines, this electorate was ex-
ploited by narrow financial interests, but even more by gross
manipulation of the democratic process.

Perez has been described as a "benevolent dictator" by his
friend, Representative Hébert (who adds, "This country needs
more like him—from the top to the bottom"). Louisiana politics is traditionally ruthless and highly professional, and Perez
belonged to the tradition, but he brought to it a particularly
aggressive style, unhampered by either subjective or purely
moral considerations. He represented much of what was wrong
with the South and much of what was revered; his lifelong defiance of higher authority made him one of the most flamboyant

5

fascinating, and outrageous political figures of twentieth-century America.

Perez resisted a Louisiana governor's political appointment in Plaquemines, an act which led to a full-scale invasion of the parish by the state militia. He was excommunicated by the Catholic Church for his outspoken defense of segregation and for exhorting others to actively oppose school desegregation. He had an incisive legal mind and sound business and political instincts, but was incapable of viewing himself or his role as public servant with any detachment. In the beginning politics meant to him acquisition in the course of perpetuation; later he accepted the role of absolute parish leader as God-given. Perez was a constant churchgoer (even after excommunication), but he was capable of outrageous manipulation of people, offices, and funds. Though his power was absolute, he lacked social pretension or a desire for celebrity outside his region. His ardent denunciation of blacks as "burr-heads" and of civil rights advocates everywhere as Communists can best be understood as a symbolic gesture of defiance toward a federal government that attempted during most of his reign to gain control of the immensely lucrative "tidelands" oil reserves.

Most of what has been written about Leander Perez is characterized by outrage, and the desperation felt by those forced to deal with the incredible. Robert Sherrill probably came closest to an appreciation of the Perez phenomenon when he wrote in *Gothic Politics in the Deep South*: "To consider Perez as a man possessed by demons is . . . to abuse him; actually his fault is in being a living caricature of Deep South officialdom, the prototype of which is not insane but merely, in turn, a caricature of sanity." His rhetoric was of the kind first proliferated by such demagogues as Benjamin Tillmann, James Vardaman, and Thomas Edward Watson, which used the race question to obscure real issues and greatly contributed to the stultification of the South in general—the sort of oratory Ralph McGill has called "magnificent irrelevancy." At times Perez appeared to be a kind of anachronistic twentieth-century demijohn in which the meaner distillation of the South's collective unconscious resided. He represented the last stand—perhaps the epitome—of the "good ole boy" as superbigot, the crusading defender of a romantic way of life that was fanciful in his own lifetime and probably never actually existed at all.

Yet he was also dynamic and intensely alive. He survived in a land where the sole objective of any contest was to win. T. Harry Williams said in his biography of Huey Long that in no state but Louisiana "were the devices employed to win— stratagems, deals, oratory—so studied and admired by the populace. It had been like this in the antebellum era, it was like this in [Henry Clay] Warmoth's time, and it would be like this in the future. . . . it is undeniable that Louisianians have always had a non-American attitude toward corruption. They have accepted it as a necessary part of political life, and they have admired it when it is executed with style and, above all, with a jest." A. J. Liebling referred to Louisiana in his *The Earl of Louisiana* as the westernmost of the Arab states, claiming that the southern part of the state in particular was part of the eastern Mediterranean littoral. "Louisiana politics," he wrote, "is of an intensity and complexity that are matched, in my experience, only in the Republic of Lebanon."

During the forty years that Perez ruled as district attorney of Plaquemines, he employed mercenary Texas gunmen and trappers to combat his own constituents in a dispute over trapping lands he had obtained, in which he organized land companies and then arranged for them to be assigned leases to extensive public lands—often over rich mineral deposits. He suppressed opposition to his machine, and transformed the local government so that the people's representation was halved and his family's perpetuation in power assured.

He was a leader in the states' rights (Dixiecrat) revolt within the Democratic party in 1948 and the major reactionary force within Louisiana's Democratic organization, always operating behind the scenes, out of the public view. Though never even a representative to the state legislature, he wrote an unreckonable amount of legislation for presentation by men

7

he controlled in the capital, Baton Rouge. He and a few inti-
mates organized the Citizens Councils in Louisiana; he constructed a concentration camp in a remote marsh for any civil
rights workers who came into Plaquemines; he offered considerable vocal and financial support to George Wallace in his
attempts to become President of the United States.

And yet Perez considered himself a "gentleman," personify-
ing the alliance between big planters and businessmen that
dominated Louisiana politics from the beginning of the nineteenth century to the time of Huey Long, and that did not die
with the Kingfish. It was this alliance that had enabled Louisiana, alone among Southern states in 1852, to adopt total population as the basis for representation in both houses of the
legislature, greatly benefiting the white planters of the Black
Belt, where Negroes counted as bodies but could not, of
course, vote.

"Louisiana was governed by gentlemen," wrote Roger W.
Shugg in his *Origins of Class Struggle in Louisiana.* "It made
no great difference to the majority of people whether power
belonged to . . . Democrats or Whigs, the country or the
city. . . . While the planters held the upper hand, filled many
offices, and set the tone of public opinion, city lawyers occupied the larger share of offices, represented the merchants, and
withal served their planting clients as well. . . . Louisiana was,
truth to tell, a slave state policed by gentlemen; and the
masses, having no real voice in government, received from it no
benefit."

Perez was a "gentleman" only in the sense that he perpetuated the planter mentality. In private, he could be charming in
the hale, courtly tradition of the nineteenth-century South; but
when speaking out against political adversaries or their policies that threatened his financial sovereignty in Plaquemines
—or against desegregation—he was more than capable of
magnificent irrelevancy. During his lifetime only a handful
of black and colored people voted in the parish, where they
made up a third of the population; he was proud of Plaquemines's tripartite segregation, with separate schools and

8

churches for whites, blacks, and mulattoes. If oil is substituted for sugar cane or cotton as the staple of the land, then the planter-merchant analogy becomes plain. As a lawyer and public official and the controller of public lands, Perez could, and did, enter into mutually advantageous agreements with the moneymen—i.e., the oil, gas, and sulphur suppliers—to the general exclusion of the interests of the people. Local government fulfilled the function of overseer. And for years Perez himself even played the role of absentee landlord, living in a mansion on Newcomb Boulevard in affluent uptown New Orleans while serving as district attorney of Plaquemines, and descending into the parish only to do business, or to hunt and fish.

Perez's concern with the supposed evils of integration, and with an international Communist conspiracy led by "Zionists," became obsessive in later life. His vision of himself as the bulwark against such "threats" grew megalomaniacal—he often referred to himself in the invincible third person—and his tolerance of any kind of opposition, nil. His followers, including many state legislators, several United States congressmen, governors, and big businessmen, were and still are intensely loyal. To some, the name Perez is holy.

. . . and Morass

A deep and fast-moving Mississippi River winds down through more than one hundred miles of low swampy country stretching south from the city of New Orleans to the Gulf. This area is Plaquemines Parish. Firm ground makes up only a small percentage of the one thousand square miles of land appearing on maps; the points of greatest elevation are the spines of the levees channeling the river toward its dissipation into the sea through half a dozen passes, and those of the back levees built to withstand the tide that sweeps in across miles of salt marsh. Long after the continent was formed, the silhouette of Plaquemines lay submerged. Gradually the Mississippi deposited sufficient silt to raise the crooked finger of spongy earth just above the waves, where it remained—a semitropical, near-primordial world of cottonwood and palmetto, sawgrass, wild cane, and cypress, floating above oil, sulphur, and natural gas deposits of almost incredible abundance, subject to floods, high winds, and a sun of African intensity.

Geographically, socially, and politically, the parish has little in common with the rest of the territorial United States. "The wildness and desolation will ever remain deeply engraved in my memory," wrote Colonel James Creecy in 1860, recalling a visit to the interior ten years before. ". . . So waste, so uninhabitable, so lonely, so like the Great Desert of the Sahara, in monotony and dreamy stillness—a dreary home for alligators, mud turtles, catfish and sea birds."

But a compatriot, John William De Forest, a captain in the Union Army, described a different view of the Plaquemines of 1862 in his A Volunteer's Adventures: "We had a charming sail from Fort Jackson to New Orleans through scenery which surpasses the Connecticut River Valley and is not inferior to that of the Hudson, though quite different in character. . . . It is a continuous flat, generally below the level of the Mississippi, but richly beautiful and full of variety. The windings of the mighty river, the endless cypress forests in the background, the vast fields of cane and corn, the abundant magnolias and orange groves and bananas, the plantation houses showing white through dark green foliage furnished an uninterrupted succession of lovely pictures."

Indians—probably Tchefunctes—making incursions into the lower Mississippi delta had once settled tentatively on the edge of the bog, but the area was too inhospitable for permanent villages, and they left behind only occasional shell mounds. La Salle planted his cross in Plaquemines, near the present town of Venice, and claimed the river valley for France in 1682. The French were the first settlers, and the parish remained largely Francophile and Catholic, although the French represented only one of several strong and independent European communities. (Plaquemines lies to the east of Louisiana's traditional Cajun country, populated by the descendants of the Acadians who migrated there in the mid-eighteenth century.) Canary Islanders arrived shortly after the French, and settled in what became Plaquemines or neighboring St. Bernard Parish to the east; they were followed by south European Slavs, Germans, Italians, Irish, Portuguese, English, Danes, Swedes, and Greeks, by Spanish-speaking Filipinos, and by Chinese, Malays, and Negroes.

A. M. Gibson, a journalist and traveler, wrote of littoral Louisiana at the end of the Civil War, "A race of mixed blood, the product of various Latin progenitors, live on the islands and along the coast of the Gulf, who are termed Dagos. They are fruiters and fishermen. For a few dollars many of them can be hired to wield the assassin's knife." Negro slaves brought in to work the sugar cane plantations were often the dangerous or unruly blacks who according to custom were "sold south," and there eventually grew up exclusive communities of mulattoes and quadroons. The Spanish and Italians became truck farmers, the Dalmatians took over the arduous oyster trade, and the poor Irish constructed the early levees, because slave labor was too valuable to spare.

Voting patterns were erratic until 1846, after which time the parish turned, and remained, consistently Democratic—an indication of voting fraud. In *Political Tendencies in Louisiana, 1812–1952*, Perry H. Howard says that "an investigation of the bloc voting in St. Bernard and Plaquemines parishes . . . would appear to be a major study in itself in view of the persistency of this phenomenon, even in the twentieth century." In the late 1800's it was common practice for boatloads of loyal voters to travel down the Mississippi, casting votes at every polling place.

In the election of 1872 all the polling places in Plaquemines were distributed south of Pointe a la Hache, the parish seat, where whites were settled, and were inaccessible to blacks living in the northern part of the parish. Residents of St. Bernard had to travel an average of fourteen miles over difficult terrain in order to vote, and the locations of many polling places were kept secret. Republicans sometimes used affidavits to obtain votes after an election. A man identified only as Jacques, who collected these affidavits, told a congressional investigating committee that his returns were mythical, and added that forgery was common. "If a man signs another man's name for the sake of money or anything of that kind, then we look upon that as forgery, but it is not so in political matters."

For the next century, Plaquemines and St. Bernard—which together comprise Louisiana's Twenty-fifth Judicial District, and share a district attorney, the office in which power is centered—were known as the state's "rotten boroughs" because of bloc voting and a particularly ruthless style of politics. More than twenty years ago, V. O. Key, Jr., in his *Southern Politics*, described Plaquemines as "an autonomous principality." In *Huey Long*, T. Harry Williams said that the leaders of St. Bernard and Plaquemines "were not politicians in the ordinary sense of the word. They were more like *caudillos* in a Latin country. They might on occasion cajole, but they usually issued genial orders. [Leander] Perez in later years would become the boss of the two parishes and would be called their dictator."

The northern boundaries of the two adjacent parishes lie just below New Orleans. Highway 39 dips south along the east bank of the Mississippi, stringing together little river towns with curious names—Arabi, Chalmette, Story—that belie a littered wayside lined with gas stations and clapboard barrooms offering fresh oysters and crabs and icy drafts of beer. At Caernovan the road crosses from St. Bernard to Plaquemines and skirts the levee across an alluvial pastoral plain: orchards of kumquat and mandarin alternate with fields of Brahman and Charolais cattle—the latter being ghostly Swiss hybrids able to withstand the humidity and the heat and the clouds of insects. Raised planters' cottages and weathered shotgun houses riding cement blocks are backed by a wall of cypress and live oak hung with Spanish moss. A dead armadillo sprawls at the edge of the narrow road, antediluvian underside exposed, tiny eyes locked into a fanatic's vision of noon, while vultures rise reluctantly from its side and settle onto the telephone lines.

Pointe a la Hache is the site of the parish's brick and stucco colonial courthouse, which has a tile roof and a diminutive clock tower facing west across the Mississippi. On the opposite bank, Highway 23 passes through towns nestled between the front and back levees, with names alternately idyllic and harshly real: Magnolia, Diamond, Happy Jack, Potash, Home Place, Empire. Trailers, many of them plugged with air conditioners and television antennas, are as numerous as houses; they are the homes of victims of the most recent hurricanes. The road ends below Venice at the "Jump," and further travel requires a boat. The town is populated by fishermen and a few trappers, and by laborers in the sprawling tank farms belonging to Gulf, Humble, and Getty, where Plaquemines's crude oil is stored before being pumped north out of the parish. The polished steel cylinders and tanks tower above a poor though ordered community that seems to embody—in spite of the neon beer signs and the pickup trucks (a bumper sticker reads, "John 3:16—Tells It Like It Is"), and the trawlers with electric winches—a pre-industrial simplicity.

The feeling of separateness in Plaquemines hasn't changed much since Perez was born. His father, Roselius Perez, was a planter and plantation overseer; descended from early Spanish settlers, Roselius proudly proclaimed himself Creole, a term used in southern Louisiana to describe early French and Spanish colonial families, and not associated with race. He grew enough rice, sugar cane, and citrus fruit to support thirteen children; he was also a politician and belonged to the Police Jury—the local governing body in Plaquemines—and to the Lafourche Levee Board and the Democratic executive committee. Roselius Perez seems to have been drawn toward politics out of a sense of responsibility more than a desire for personal gain, though he later became involved in some of his son's political maneuvers.

Leander Henry was his seventh child, born in 1891. He attended the proverbial one-room schoolhouse in Plaquemines, where his older sister was his teacher. He assisted in the maintenance of his father's small plantation, fished and shot ducks along the bayous and endless salt marshes, watched the ocean freighters steaming up from Pilottown at the river's mouth. The family was staunchly Catholic, and when Perez was old enough he was encouraged to attend the strongly parochial Holy Cross College in New Orleans, a respectable training ground for most Catholic heirs in the area.

Many of his classmates were far better off than he. Perez transferred to Louisiana State University in Baton Rouge, where he worked part-time as a waiter in the cafeteria, joined every student organization he could, played the bass horn in two different bands, and was a member of the football team. He was elected secretary of the Athletic Association, and class salutatorian. The school yearbook, the *Gumbo*, said of him: "He is a paralyzer of the female heart." While living in the state capital, Perez began to attend state legislative sessions; in 1912, he became a secretary for the appropriations committee. Much later, he became known as the legislature's "third house," for over the next half-century he missed few if any legislative sessions, and there came to be a kind of gentlemen's agreement among succeeding governors that Louisiana's legislature could not open unless Judge Perez was on hand.

In 1914, Perez graduated from Tulane University Law School. In the yearbook section entitled "What the '14 Law Class Likes" it is revealed that Perez "likes politics." The yearbook photograph shows a short, sturdy young man in a high starched collar, button shoes, and a large stickpin, confronting the camera as if it were an adversary. His hair is already combed into the pompadour that was to become more rampant as he grew older; he already wears the metal-rimmed hexagonal spectacles; he seems intent, yet undeniably skeptical.

With a fellow law school graduate, Perez rented an office in New Orleans and tried unsuccessfully to build up a successful practice. In 1916, he received his first opportunity to run for office, and took it, though it was generally accepted that he had no chance of winning. As a candidate for state legislator from Plaquemines, he opposed an entrenched political faction that had run the parish since shortly after Reconstruction. His father was no longer a political power; Perez's candidacy was considered futile and even dangerous, since opposition candidates were often harassed and beaten when apprehended in the parish's wilder regions. But Perez recognized the opportunity to establish his reputation both in Plaquemines and in Baton Rouge, where political appointments were made.

Although the vast majority of Louisiana voters were registered as Democrats, and election outcomes were determined in practice in the primaries, a strong bi-factionalism did exist within the state Democratic party, and at times this split caused it to function virtually as a two-party system. Candidates for governor from each of the opposing factions would run entire slates of candidates for minor offices, even down to the local level. There existed no single state machine, but each parish had a ruling courthouse clique, usually controlled by the sheriff, who would decide which candidates the clique would support and who was relied upon to deliver a certain percentage of the vote in each election. The objective of each gubernatorial candidate was to line up as many sheriffs as possible, since they were the most powerful local figures and embodied the basic authority of government. And opposing the ruling clique in each parish was the clique on the outside, trying to get into power.

Perez perceived his greatest opportunity in opposition, rather than in trying to work his way into the rigidly controlled courthouse clique. He ran as a "good government" candidate, attacking controlled elections. He walked along the tops of the levees and solicited boat rides, staying in plain view and haranguing Plaquemines voters about the necessity to preserve their individual rights. He avoided trouble, managed to poll a handful of votes, and gained a reputation for intelligence and guts. Equally important, his candidacy was an aggressive and definitive gesture that aligned him with the parish's "reform" faction, and would provide him with his first political position.

After the outbreak of World War I, Perez—newly married to Agnes Chalin of New Orleans—enrolled in officer's candidate school, but he received an honorable discharge without ever seeing action. By 1919 he was still sitting in his New Orleans law office, and still poor; he was already well acquainted with politics, both in Plaquemines and in Baton Rouge, and he knew that many men less intelligent and ambitious than he were prospering in elected offices. He seemed relegated to a meager, uneventful existence. Then the district judge of Plaquemines drowned while on a fishing trip; and Perez was suggested to fill the vacant post.

It was common practice in the Twenty-fifth Judicial District to select a district attorney from one of the two parishes that composed it, and a judge from the other. The new governor, John M. Parker, had run as a reformer, and had been opposed by the local regulars; in 1919 the district attorney was from St. Bernard, and Leander Perez was one of the few attorneys from Plaquemines who had aligned himself with the reform faction. He accepted Parker's offer of the judgeship, to be filled until the next election a year away. Always a pragmatist, Perez viewed politics as a profession, and was willing and able to develop any advantage. One succeeded by moving up through the ranks, always bettering his position. It was a calculated approach—that of an astute businessman and accountant, rather than of a charismatic public figure. And in 1919 the circumstances were right for the beginning of his ascent.

On the Monday morning following the elected judge's drowning, Perez arrived at the courthouse to be sworn in. However, he found the doors locked: the ruling clique had declared a holiday, and its leaders had managed to get the state supreme court to appoint an *ad hoc* judge from their own ranks. Unimpressed, Perez had himself sworn in on the courthouse lawn. He traveled upriver to the St. Bernard courthouse and repeated the ceremony in similar fashion, since that building too was locked.

The state supreme court eventually had to decide which of the two contenders was the rightful district court judge. Perez, only twenty-eight years old, presented his own case to the court. He argued that according to Louisiana's constitution, if an elective office is vacated with less than one year remaining in its term, the governor has the right to appoint a successor. A majority of the court agreed with his argument, and he assumed the title of "Judge" that he would retain for the rest of his life.

Perez's chances of being elected to a full four-year term in the next election seemed negligible. He had almost no support within the courthouse when he took over the bench; the ruling clique was accustomed to providing at least 90 per cent of the vote for its own candidates. Perez ignored those holding elected offices within the two parishes, and concentrated on members of the grand jury, over whom he had some power. By carefully grooming the jury, he was able by election time to make effective use of the threat of indictment for engaging in election fraud. In the Twenty-fifth Judicial District, such fraud varied from simple forgery to intimidation by partisan poll watchers to the actual dumping of acid into ballot boxes known to contain a high percentage of opposition votes. But Perez's threat worked. He was elected by a plurality of three votes, and his candidate for district attorney, Philip Livaudais, also won.

As judge, Perez behaved flamboyantly, even by Plaquemines standards. He kept a pearl-handled revolver in plain view on the bench; he used his judgeship itself as an offensive weapon, performing as well the duties of prosecutor and investigator. Since most of his enemies lived in St. Bernard, he attacked that parish's two biggest industries, gambling and rumrunning. He frequently fixed cases for trial without consulting the district attorney; consequently he and Livaudais soon split. Once Perez allowed four of his own friends charged with falsifying election returns to waive trial by jury, and promptly found them innocent. He even ordered a St. Bernard petit jury to dine at a restaurant owned by a man who was pro-Perez, the juries having been accustomed to dining in an establishment operated by a partisan of the opposition. He began as well to extend his influence in other directions, regularly attending meetings of the levee board and the Plaquemines school board, both of which controlled leases to extensive public lands; at meetings of the latter, he was often observed passing notes to his brother, a board member.

Soon he found himself in his first political battle: Livaudais, with other members of the parish's anti-Perez faction, filed suit in the state supreme court to have the judge removed from the bench, charging him with official misconduct, favoritism, and oppression. Perez called them "a bunch of dummies with no guts" (a phrase he often used to castigate uncooperative grand juries), and sought to link the petitioners with gambling in St. Bernard. "As judge of this district I closed those gambling houses. I sent some of the gamblers and corrupt officials to jail, and there still remains some exposure to be made. Some of these officials know that I stand in their way to reap large returns, and therefore they would like to have me removed."

Livaudais denounced Perez as "a little political upstart"; Perez called Livaudais "a tool of those professional politicians. . . . This situation brings out forcibly [the proof] that when a man fools with dirt, he cannot expect anything but mudslinging."

The impeachment proceedings in Baton Rouge were well covered in the newspapers. They lasted many months, and proved nothing. Another election was approaching in which Perez intended to run for the position of real power, that of district attorney, and as in all elections there were deals to be made and new alliances to be formed. One morning, therefore, he agreed to withdraw his own statements made "in the heat of a political campaign," if the charges against him were dropped. The charges were dropped, and one witness compared the truce to "the courtship dance of the whooping cranes."

The proceedings had only strengthened Perez's position, and he was elected district attorney for Plaquemines and St. Bernard. That same year, 1924, he had to borrow money from his mother-in-law to pay $6,500 for Promised Land, a house on the east bank of the river. He moved in with his wife and children, and set himself up as befitted the single most powerful figure in Plaquemines. He was thirty-three years old.

Huey Long and Leander Perez wouldn't seem to have had much in common. Long was born and raised in Winn Parish, a hilly land of inferior soil in the Protestant northern part of Louisiana, land which was poor and unsuited to the sugar cane and cotton plantations of the lowlands. Northern Louisianans were traditionally suspicious of the more sophisticated, prosperous, Francophile Catholics who populated the bottom of the state; and the Catholics cared little for the rednecks from the north. But both Long and Perez were the products of large and relatively poor families, and both were inordinately ambitious, bright, gutsy, arrogant, and highly vituperative on the attack. Also, both understood how Louisiana politics worked, and were able to act on their decisions. Most important, they were both associated with the reform faction when they entered politics, and both opposed the New Orleans Old Regular machine. The head of that machine, and New Orleans' perennial mayor, was a man named Martin Behrman, who supposedly once said, "You can make prostitution illegal in Louisiana, but you can't make it unpopular."

In June 1921, Perez wrote a letter to Governor Parker requesting the dismissal of a political rival from the examiners board of the Mississippi River Pilots' Association. "Unfortunately," Perez wrote, "like most state boards in the past, the Behrmanizing process of rewarding the faithful and persecuting the free and independent thinkers has been fast demoralizing the men and affecting the service. . . . The pilots who supported you, and the anti-ring people of this Parish generally, feel that they have experienced the same burdens under the old ring system as did the people of New Orleans."

As Perez and Long—then railroad commissioner, and an ally of the governor—were thus both openly committed to the defeat of the New Orleans ring, they began to depend on one another to help advance their respective careers. Long lost his first governor's race in 1924, the year of the impeachment proceedings against Perez, but four years later he won with a heavy upstate vote combined with much of the vote in the extreme southern parishes, including Plaquemines and St. Bernard, which Perez had helped to deliver.

Thus, with a friendly governor in office, Perez was bound to prosper. By obtaining from Long favorable local appointments —particularly to the levee boards, which controlled rights to lands under which oil and sulphur were discovered—Perez was able to control what proved to be almost incredibly large assets. Perez's activities would occasionally prove embarrassing to Huey, who once told him, "Sometimes I wish I could cut Plaquemines loose and let it drift out into the Gulf."

"I wish you could," Perez replied.

Chapter
Two

Oiling
the
Machine

Believe it or not, I'm a reformer at heart.
Leander Perez

Pay Dirt

As early as 1926, Perez was becoming involved in land deals in Plaquemines. He established his own land companies "for the purpose of taking up some leases." The two biggest and most enduring were Delta Development and Louisiana Coastal, which obtained their leases either directly from the levee boards, or by assignment from other parties who had obtained the leases from the levee boards and then re-leased the land to the oil companies.

Control of the levee boards was essential to control of the parish. The boards were originally organized simply to construct levees, an important function in an area so susceptible to flooding. Marsh lands were assigned by the state to the levee boards for use in raising money for the building and maintenance of these levees. Lands forfeited to the state for unpaid taxes were also assigned to the boards (more than one trapper in Plaquemines complained of being encouraged by politicians not to pay taxes on his land, which thus would eventually be declared forfeited and reassigned to one of the levee boards).

Board members were appointed by the governor. Perez arranged the passage of a constitutional amendment (all new laws in Louisiana, which operates on the French legal system, amend the constitution) allowing the local governing body, the Police Jury, to assume the indebtedness of any board within parish boundaries, a move apparently intended to assist in the maintenance of public lands. Actually, it was a brilliant maneuver because it also meant that the Police Jury assumed the boards' assets—and over the next twenty years these assets totaled more than $200 million in oil and sulphur production. Perez, as district attorney, headed the Police Jury.

Land leases might be obtained relatively cheaply by the oil companies and sulphur developers, but these companies would have to agree to pay what was known as an "over-riding royalty"—a fixed percentage of the amount of production of oil or sulphur. By the early 1930's it was already apparent to mineral developers trying to get a foothold in Plaquemines that the leases with the most powerful backing came from Delta Development and Louisiana Coastal. Associates of Perez served as officers for both companies, and he himself acted as their attorney; significantly, the attorney's fees of both companies often equaled approximately half their yearly income.

In terms of oil deposits, Plaquemines was to prove the richest parish in Louisiana, itself one of the largest oil-producing states; Plaquemines also contained the second largest sulphur dome in the world. The scramble for land was furious and often devious, and the history of a particular lease could become as difficult to follow as a nutria's trail through sawgrass. And Perez was particularly adept at camouflaging the trail.

In 1932 seven hundred acres of land came up for sale for unpaid taxes. The owners of the land were unknown, and according to law a notice of the sale had to be published in the official parish journal, the Plaquemines *Gazette*. The editor of the *Gazette* was J. Ben Meyer, a Plaquemines-style intellectual with an amateur's interest in local history and a real interest in politics, who over the years was to swing back and forth between the Perez faction and their adversaries. In 1932 Meyer belonged to the ruling clique; he admits that on Perez's instructions he wrote to the Western Newspaper Union in Memphis, Tennessee, where much of the *Gazette's* printing was done, instructing that one hundred extra editions be printed incorporating the notice of the land sale. The regular editions of the paper, however, were not to mention the sale. The notice appeared in specially printed copies of the *Gazette* for December 3, 10, 17, 24, and 31, and January 7, 1933. These issues were hidden for six weeks—until after the sale—and then placed in the sheriff's files to prove that the sale had been advertised. The land was sold without competitive bidding to Robert J. Lobrano, a legal associate of Perez's whose name appears repeatedly in connection with land deals in Plaquemines.

In another instance, Perez discovered a mistake in the survey for a township in the area of Lake Grande Ecaille, later to produce millions of dollars in oil and sulphur. The Buras levee board had control of land on the west bank of the Mississippi, but the state retained the rights to the water bottoms; the boundary was extremely variable, since a survey made in the autumn would assign considerably more land to the levee board than one made during the spring floods. The township near Lake Grande Ecaille had been established three miles too far north, and included in what was called the Payne Plats. This area, upon which the levee board based its land sale, fitted two townships into a space large enough for only a township and a half, and consequently all section boundaries were fictitious.

Perez filed suit for the levee board against the owners of the disputed land. He claimed certain sections of new land for the board, and replotted the two townships. The state supreme court, after hearing the case, observed that the disputed sections "have been, figuratively speaking, pulled down south more than a mile from where the Payne map locates them, and incidentally pulled out of the water and onto land and placed on the exact spot where oil was discovered."

The court decided that the Buras levee board did not own the oil dome. Perez filed another suit in the court of appeals—where he had more influence—and obtained the less damaging decision that the title to the disputed sections of the township "as it is actually located is settled, but no other land is covered by the decree." In other words, no one knew exactly where the disputed sections were, despite the supreme court ruling. Years later an oil man recalled, "We [Humble, Gulf, Shell] were all floating around. The only way we could handle it was to pool our leases and work out compromise agreements."

The same deal involved Freeport Sulphur, which moved into Plaquemines confident that it would be the dominant force in the parish, and soon discovered that it had three and a half million dollars invested in a mining operation on land of unknown ownership. The situation is worth examining in detail because it illustrates the almost incredible complexity of land deals in Plaquemines, and the manner in which Perez was able to obtain his own objectives.

In 1928 an ex-soldier and gambler, Colonel Robert Morris, made a list of state-owned lands in southern Plaquemines near sites where oil and sulphur had been discovered. He presented the list to the Buras levee board, and suggested that it ask the state to grant it these lands. The members were so appreciative that after the state had fulfilled the request, they granted a mineral lease on 11,000 newly acquired acres to an associate of Colonel Morris's. The lease included a tract of 320 acres called Fractional Section One, which contained one of the largest sulphur deposits in the world. For good form's sake the lease was transferred to another of Morris's associates, Herbert Waguespack, who then assigned the precious Fractional Section One to Morris.

The deal attracted Perez's attention. He studied the map, discovered a mistake in the original and subsequent surveys, and had his own survey done. He then suggested that Fractional Section One might be included among the "lost" lands to be handed back to the levee board, which had come under his control. Without waiting for the board to acquire title officially, he suggested that it lease these additional "lost" lands to Robert Lobrano. Perez argued that their exact location could be shown later in a supplemental lease, and Lobrano obtained more than nine thousand acres of extremely valuable land. But he paid only five hundred dollars annual rent. He also agreed to pay the levee board fifty cents a ton in royalties on all sul-

phur mined, and a one-eighth royalty on all oil produced. Lobrano's lease at this point made no specific claim to Fractional
Section One, still supposedly under Colonel Morris's control,
but only to nine thousand "lost" acres.

In May 1930, Lobrano assigned his lease to the Gulf Refining Company in return for twenty-five cents a ton in over-riding
royalties on all sulphur produced within the nine thousand
acres (the over-ride meant that Gulf paid an additional twenty-
five cents a ton to the lessor, and assumed all other obligations
under the lease granted by the levee board). The board—
represented by Perez—intervened in Lobrano's transaction and
stipulated that the lease included parts of Fractional Section
One not included in the original lease. Two years later, Colonel
Morris agreed to assign his lease on Fractional Section One to
Lobrano, who then had total claim to the land. Waguespack
still had possession of the earlier lease, and contested Lobrano's and the levee board's claim. The affair eventually went to
court, where it lodged.

Freeport Sulphur, in the meantime, had millions of dollars
tied up in Fractional Section One. The company therefore refused to pay royalties to anyone—Lobrano, the Buras levee
board, or Waguespack—until the matter was settled, and
thereby began a losing battle with Judge Perez. Freeport ini-
tially had made the mistake of considering Plaquemines to be a
one-company parish, with itself as sole proprietor. It not only
held up royalty payments, but laid off workers from Plaquemines and began bringing in employees from outside the
parish.

While Perez was in Baton Rouge keeping track of the "lost"
lands proceedings in court (he officially represented the levee
board), he arranged the passage of a legislative bill proposing
to raise the severance tax on sulphur from sixty cents to two
dollars a long ton. Freeport's president, Langbourne Williams,
hurried to Baton Rouge and went directly to the new governor,
Richard Leche, a member of the Long organization who once
said, "When I took the oath as governor, I didn't take any vows
of poverty." Leche assured Williams that Perez's severance tax

bill would be vetoed, and then almost immediately signed the bill into law.

Freeport was faced with a 233 per cent tax raise, all because of Perez, the man whose parish was supposed to benefit most from Freeport's activities. It could cut back sulphur production by one-fourth but no more, because Plaquemines supplied more than half of Freeport's total output. The tax couldn't possibly be lowered until the legislature met again, and Freeport had nothing to lose by fighting Perez. In an attempt to have him ousted, Freeport founded a rival newspaper, the Plaquemines *Times*, and convinced the quixotic Ben Meyer, who had recently joined the ranks of the opposing faction, to be its editor. Meyer sniped at Perez for almost two years, without much effect. By the time the legislature was scheduled to meet again, Freeport was ready to make concessions.

Perez made all the arrangements. First he agreed to keep the overall property tax rate in Plaquemines below twenty mills, if Freeport agreed to employ a certain percentage of Plaquemines residents. He then maneuvered through the new legislature another bill reducing the severance tax on sulphur to $1.03 a long ton. Leche approved the 48 per cent reduction just as promptly as he had approved the 233 per cent increase. (Meyer said years later, "Freeport paid him off. That's how that stuff got done.") Second, Perez advised the Buras levee board to accept an offer by Freeport to it and to Lobrano and Waguespack of $.25 on sulphur produced prior to 1938, and $.35 a long ton on sulphur produced after that year. Predictably, the recommendation was accepted, as well as Perez's formula of how the sulphur package was to be divided.

In the final arrangement the levee board—the public body —didn't get the fifty cents a long ton specified in the original contract. It received only 32 per cent of that amount for production before 1938, and 40 per cent for production thereafter. Lobrano (Perez's man) and Waguespack as individual litigants received a slightly larger cut of the pre-1938 royalties than the levee board, and a considerably larger cut of the 60 per cent on future royalties. Lobrano and Waguespack each received roughly the same portions of pre-1938 royalties, but in future payments Lobrano, according to Perez's agreement, could receive as much as five times that received by Waguespack or the levee board.

In his article in *Fortune* magazine about land deals in Plaquemines, Richard Austin Smith asked the rhetorical question, "Who was Robert J. Lobrano? . . . As the Judge explained, [Lobrano] was 'one of our boys.' He might better be described as Perez' boy, the nominee who had been trading in levee board mineral leases since the Twenties. . . . As an officer of Delta Development, Lobrano was to witness the 1936 lease whereby Delta got oil, gas and mineral rights on a tract of land (estimated at 10,000 to 30,000 acres) from the Grand Prairie Levee Board [east bank of the Mississippi in Plaquemines] for no more than 3¢ an acre (even then the going price in the coastal parishes, according to an expert opinion, was $1 to $3 an acre). Now, after the sulphur settlement, Lobrano turned around and assigned to Louisiana Coastal, one of the other land companies Perez had organized, $32,263 of his $43,017 cash settlement and all but 3¼ cents of his future royalties. . . . In consideration of this assignment he was paid 500 shares of Louisiana Coastal. But who was Louisiana Coastal? Lobrano, Coastal's president from 1939 to 1941, said it was Judge Perez."

After the agreement between Perez and Freeport, the actual ownership of disputed land became unimportant as an issue. Perez was the undisputed power in the parish; Freeport treated him with the deference any foreign investor gives to the ruler of the nation in which it is investing. In January 1939, Freeport's vice president, J. T. Claiborne, Jr., wrote to Perez from New York: "I can't tell you how much I enjoyed my whole trip. You were a perfect host in every way, and I never had better sport. The only regrettable part about the whole trip is that, upon returning, I have not found it possible to exaggerate about the number of geese and ducks I saw and had shots at. . . . I should appreciate your telling Robert Lobrano . . . that I am looking forward to seeing [him and his wife] here in New York. I am still in hopes that they will be able to induce you and Mrs. Perez to accompany them."

In 1924 Perez had had to borrow money to buy his home, Promised Land. His salary over the next fifteen years was approximately seven thousand dollars annually. Shortly after the settlement with Freeport, the Judge boasted to friends that he had made his first million.

Perez's dealings with the oil companies were just as Byzantine. When Earl Long, Huey's brother, later became governor, he looked into land deals in Plaquemines, and told an associate, "As the chief executive of this state I thought I had a right to look at income taxes. . . . I found several astonishing revelations. I found that a certain district attorney had gone, I think, from $24,000 . . . to $200,000. . . . I'm informed that the levee boards in Plaquemines Parish, and some companies that a certain man [is] interested in, are receiving royalties from the Freeport Sulphur Company. I'm informed that that's not necessarily a voluntary contribution. . . . If you want to do well, you've got to stay with the King. I had a man the other day tell me—[he's] a multi-millionaire—that he swore he would not give an over-riding royalty. . . . He stood out and stood out and finally his partners came to him and said, 'Listen, we've got some great investments. Everybody else in that part of the country has done it. Go ahead and do it, and let's recover something on our investment.' "

The "King" was, of course, Perez. By the mid-1940's Plaquemines was producing 10 per cent more oil than any other parish in Louisiana: about eighteen million barrels annually, worth some forty million dollars, and another twenty million dollars' worth of sulphur. Perez was legal adviser to the Police Jury, the levee and school boards, and the most powerful land companies; in this capacity he acted as a shrewd accountant rather than a political figure, and kept most transactions technically legal. His public and private duties were so intertwined that for years his New Orleans law offices and a levee board shared the same phone number (the levee board paid the bill). Royalty rights on public land leased in Plaquemines would be assigned to companies for which Perez was the lawyer; he could thus negotiate for both sides, draw up the contracts, have them notarized by his associate, and witnessed by his secretary and the assistant district attorney.

Perez always maintained that he did not legally own the biggest companies, Louisiana Coastal and Delta Development. But friends and associates served as company officers: A. Sidney Cain, Jr., Perez's law associate, was vice president of Louisiana Coastal. Officers of Delta Development included Harold Sicard of Thomas J. Moran Sons, printers whom Perez represented legally and whom he helped obtain lucrative state printing jobs, Perez's ally Robert J. Chauvin, and Robert Lobrano of the Freeport Sulphur deal. The fact that the companies received valuable leases on public lands seemed natural to Perez, or so he said: "What reason would I have to object that my friends should have leases?"

Perez the attorney made a great deal of money. According to Louisiana tax records, Delta Development in 1938 paid $89,000—more than half its income after depletion deductions —in legal fees. (The previous year, the company authorized the purchase of health, accident, and life insurance for its officers *and* attorneys.) Chauvin's salary was only $5,000, Lobrano's only $3,600. The following year, Delta paid $76,400 in legal fees, an average of $1,460 per week, whereas the company's other expenses, including rent, averaged only about $16 per week. Lobrano and Chauvin owned only a fraction of one per cent of the stock. That year Perez reported an income of $218,000, and the oil boom was young.

An example of Delta Development's operations is that of the Grand Bay oil field. The Grand Prairie levee board leased lands in the field to Delta; the board was to receive in return a rental royalty of one-eighth of the value of oil produced. The lease was then assigned to Gulf Refining Company, with Gulf assuming all of Delta's obligations under the lease. On the same day Gulf made another agreement: to pay Perez's associate, Cain, an over-riding royalty of one-forty-eighth on the value of oil produced. Cain promptly assigned the over-riding royalty to Delta for the amazingly small sum of $150. Twelve years after the Grand Bay field began production, the barrels of oil totaled fourteen million, and Delta had made a cool $750,000.

Another example: the original lease to the West Bay oil field was obtained by Delta from the Buras Levee Board on the river's west bank. Delta agreed to pay a rental royalty of one-eighth, and an additional one-forty-eighth until the levee board had received an additional $100,000. Delta assigned the lease to Gulf, which assumed all the obligations under the lease with the notable exception that the board's one-forty-eighth additional royalty up to $100,000 was changed to one-forty-eighth *of* one-eighth. Again on the very same day, Gulf signed a contract with Cain agreeing to pay him an over-riding royalty of one-forty-eighth (less the pittance going to the levee board), and Cain promptly assigned his over-ride to Delta. In ten years West Bay produced forty million barrels of oil, and Delta received $200,000.

The levee boards—i.e., the public—received no royalty payment of any size from either of these two transactions. Literally millions of dollars flowed into the Police Jury, which in assuming the indebtedness of the parish boards had also assumed their assets, as has been shown. Perez never allowed the boards to pay off their debts, and so they remained under his control.

Oil companies dealing with Perez included Gulf, Shell, Texas, Humble, Tidewater, and California. A 135 million dollar land dispute eventually involved most of them, after John Mecom, Houston's wealthy independent oil man, took some leases on land in Plaquemines. The leases belonged to Ernest Cockrell, Jr., who had bought the land in 1927; it included part of the lucrative Lake Washington oil field. Mecom drilled two wells on the property to validate Cockrell's holdings; Cockrell and his associates were to receive 17⅞ per cent of the value of production. Mecom found that he needed more cash to develop the field, and Freeport Sulphur bought half-interest in the project.

31

Unfortunately for Mecom and Freeport, they hadn't consulted with the Judge. Perez waited until production began, and then stepped in, claiming that they were drilling on a portion of his land which had already been leased in parts to Humble, Gulf, Texas, and Shell. Mecom's representative asked Perez where his land was, and later said, "Everywhere we drilled, *that* was his land." The disputed land had originally been leased to Delta for the absurdly low figure of $1,500, while the land company could expect to make several fortunes once production was underway. Perez represented Humble and the other giants; he made what Mecom considered an "outrageous" demand, and Mecom-Freeport broke off negotiations, with Mecom apparently convinced that he would continue pumping oil until Perez decided to be reasonable.

Perez could afford to be patient. The sheriff could at his leisure halt trucks carrying essential drilling equipment for infractions of minor laws and keep them from making deliveries for days; oil companies attempting to rent boats to work the offshore rigs from companies outside the parish often found the gas tanks of those boats full of sugar. Narrow waterways leading to the rigs were just as often blocked by fishermen. Mecom-Freeport finally agreed to what appeared to be a compromise: Humble, Shell, Texas, and Gulf would receive half the value of production from the disputed lands and Delta would receive an over-ride on this money, as the sub-lessor.

Mecom-Freeport lost exactly fifty per cent of the mineral wealth from land they thought they owned. "Every oil company in the business holds leases from Delta Development," a Gulf executive admitted. "They [Perez and Delta] are pretty well synonymous." (By 1957 Plaquemines's oil production had reached $184 million annually. The year before, the Police Jury received the following mineral royalty payments: $894,000 from Gulf, $650,000 from Tidewater, $513,000 from Humble, $218,000 from Freeport, and $173,000 from California—a grand total of $2,448,000.)

Perez admitted to owning only "8,000 acres of land for about 20 years. I've leased it and don't have a well on it."

After thirty years in public office, Perez took credit for all the improvements in the parish. He boasted of $9,000,000 invested in new schools—$2,700,000 of that amount for separate facilities for Negroes and mulattoes, schools "of equal excellence." Perez distributed an average of $25,000 a year in college scholarships from parish funds. Ten thousand new farm acres had been drained. There were three new water purification and distribution plants, two main highways and many secondary roads, a free ferry, free canals, waterways and locks, and even free repairs for the boats of fishermen who voted the right ticket. Perez also boasted that Plaquemines had the lowest tax rate in the state, and probably in the country. Considering the amount of money being made from Plaquemines mineral resources by a few people, some residents thought they should *receive* regular cash installments, though few said this in front of witnesses. To complain about the actions of those in power was to invite trouble.

Helping Huey

Louisiana's rule by gentlemen—conservative planters and big city merchants in alliance—during the nineteenth century created a genuine potential for class conflict. An overt struggle failed to develop because of the preoccupation with race, fomented by politicians who catered to latent fears and avoided the real economic issues, and because of the disruptive events of Reconstruction. It was the planter-merchant alliance that led an unenthusiastic Louisiana into the Civil War, in spite of the opposition of small farmers who did not own slaves and who suspected that the war was contrary to their interests. During Reconstruction, class tensions were diluted by that "magnificent irrelevancy," the cry of racial honor, as well as by the experience common to all Louisiana whites of subjugation to Republican opportunists voted in by Negroes.

Class resentment remained mostly dormant until the rise of

Huey Pierce Long, Jr. (In the presidential election of 1912 Eugene V. Debs received five thousand votes in Louisiana, mainly from the old Populist areas.) Long's country was Populist country, dry and deprived, a natural spawning place for a leader anxious to launch welfare policies at the expense of the "gentlemen" and their interests—the corporations and the railroads.

Long was born in 1893 on a farm consisting of three hundred acres of poor soil invaded by second-growth pine. He was the eighth of nine children; he worked his way through college by peddling Cottolene, a lard product, through northern Louisiana. He completed the Tulane Law School program in less than one year, ran for a position on the Railway Commission in 1918, and won by selling himself as an anti-corporationist and a supporter of reduced utility rates. He supported Parker in 1920, but later broke with him because Parker sanctioned amendments to the bill declaring Standard Oil's pipelines to be public carriers, which had been Long's idea. By 1924, when Huey first ran for governor, he was known throughout Louisiana as a daring and irreverent opponent of the big interests.

Long's programs for wholesale road construction and free schoolbooks were a radical departure from Louisiana's traditional Bourbon concept of government; when he proposed an occupational-license, or manufacturer's, tax of five cents a barrel on the refining of crude oil, the conservatives led by Standard Oil determined to fight him. Standard's money had been used to buy off key legislators and others with influence in the state, and Long's oil tax was defeated; but the rallied forces of the opposition, many of them honestly opposed to Long's policies, and richer and bolder because of Standard's largesse, decided to go all the way: they wanted Huey impeached. Long attempted to have the legislature adjourned before impeachment proceedings could begin, but failed after his supporters and opponents battled openly on the floor of the House in the famous altercation known as "Bloody Monday." (One of the opponents was struck in the forehead and bloodied by a Longite's fist, a pair of brass knuckles, or the blade of an electric fan, depending upon the source of the account.)

The charges against Long were varied and seemingly devastating. A resolution was introduced in the House charging Long with "high crimes and misdemeanors"—nineteen in all—including a conspiracy to murder a state representative opposed to him, and an attempt to intimidate the anti-Long owner of two Baton Rouge newspapers, Charles Manship, by threatening to reveal that his brother was residing in a state mental institution. The real complaint against Huey, of course, was that he substituted the welfare of Louisiana for that of Standard Oil, and did it in such an ungentlemanly and effective manner.

The effect on Long of Bloody Monday and the subsequent impeachment proceedings was paralytic. He apparently believed that his political career was finished; his older brother Julius claims to have found him lying on his bed, sobbing and tearing at his clothes. He had no plan of defense and his organization had been weakened, but some able legislators and country supporters stayed with him.

One of these was Perez, who had himself been through the rigors of impeachment proceedings and could offer Long advice. Though he had not been a part of the Long organization, Perez acted as one of Long's chief strategists and a stanchion about which the Longites gathered to map out a battle plan; it was he who presided over the partisan caucuses of several dozen men in the old Heidelburg Hotel in Baton Rouge. Long, after his brief period of withdrawal, took the offensive, attacking Standard Oil and their legislators in hand-delivered circulars—a device he had already used previously to reach rural voters—and over the radio.

On April 6, 1929, a leader of the opposition in the House moved for a vote to impeach Long on the Manship charge with the sanctimonious words: "Such a character should, and you know it in your heart of hearts, be eliminated by the proper legal action of any further right to continue to cast disgrace on our fair State." Longite leader Allen Ellender claimed that Long might have threatened Manship, but had done so as a private individual, not in his capacity as governor, an argument dismissed by an opponent as "heifer manure."

In the confusion that followed charge and countercharge, the representative from Plaquemines Parish, a gaunt and eccentric man named George Delesdernier, stood up, apparently at Perez's bidding, and asked to address the other legislators. There followed what has been called the strangest speech in the history of a legislature that has heard many.

"Bear with me in patience while I say what I have to say," Delesdernier began. "The title of my speech will be 'The Cross of Wood and with Shackles of Paper.' Nineteen hundred years ago there was a cross of wood erected and a Divine Creature of that time was nailed to the Cross. This Divine Creature was going through the country relieving the sick and afflicted, curing the lame and the halt, aiding the deaf and the blind, and driving illiteracy from the country that surrounded Him by teaching salvation to man, woman and child. He was surrounded by a committee of twelve. There was a traitor in the ranks. Charges were preferred before a judge."

Legislators opposed to Long began to call out "Sacrilege!" and "Blasphemy!" and one attempted to invoke a House rule against sacrilegious statements. Delesdernier pointed out that he had not used the name of Christ, and continued: "The judge washed his hands of the charges as not being sustained and the mob was not satisfied with the verdict of the judge, and they took this Divine Creature and crucified Him by driving nails into His hands and feet. Today we have a creature among us who is relieving the sick and the destitute. . . ."

Again there were loud objections in the chamber, but the Speaker ruled that Delesdernier might continue. As he spoke, the shouts of protest grew steadily louder.

"Today there is a creature relieving the sick and the blind, aiding the lame and the halt, and trying to drive illiteracy from the state, and he is being shackled with paper to a cross. The cross was manufactured—one of the uprights—out of a saintly piece. The horizontal part of the cross is from the beams of the moon, and this divine creature—I mean this creature of today —is being shackled with paper...."

The uproar was such that Delesdernier couldn't go on. He shouted, "Take my life, but give me my character," and collapsed. According to one account, Delesdernier had to be carried from the chamber; another source said that he did not collapse, but carefully lay down beside the podium. After another legislator announced, "His pulse is as strong as mine," Delesdernier stood and returned to his seat.

This type of tactic was inadequate to the fervor of the opposition. The House voted to impeach on the Manship charge by a margin of eighteen votes, and the proceedings eventually moved to the Senate, which resolved itself into a court in accordance with Louisiana law. Now the Longites contended that the eighteen-day session of the legislature stipulated in the original motion had expired on April 6, after which date no charges other than the original Manship charge could lawfully be considered. A motion by the Long forces embodying this contention was defeated; fourteen senators voted for it, however—an indication of some support for Huey. There were thirty-nine senators; two-thirds of their votes—twenty-six— were needed to impeach him; if the same (or any) fourteen senators voted for acquittal, then Huey would be saved.

Either Long or Perez had an idea that was to defeat impeachment: they would draw up a document containing the names of the senators that had opposed the proceedings as unlawful because the official duration of the legislative session had expired; these men would be committed to voting against impeachment, regardless of any evidence presented by Long's enemies. The document was called the Round Robin. There were apparently two such documents, the first drafted by Ellender, each containing the names of fifteen senators who had succumbed to Huey's arguments that the Senate was entitled to try only the original Manship charge.

Perez was one of eight attorneys representing Long, but he was the only one who had himself been tried for impeachment.

He used an argument that had been used in his own defense five years before: the case of the Louisiana district judge who had fired with impunity at another man. He objected to the article of impeachment on the grounds that the charges failed to indicate any of the high crimes or misdemeanors or types of official misconduct which were "well defined in the jurisprudence of Louisiana." "In adopting this article," Perez continued, "the House was moved by heated spirit rather than by a desire to follow the provisions of the constitution. . . . Gross misconduct means official misconduct or habitual vice. Can the governor . . . or any other public official be charged with nonsense for impeachment or removal from office? By this article, it is alleged that the governor attempted to blackmail Manship, the mighty Manship. According to this article, a word from the mighty Manship would have controlled the legislature."

At that point an anti-Long representative jumped to his feet and said, "We don't charge that Manship or anyone else controls the legislature." He suggested that Perez had spoken "without thinking."

"I meant exactly what I said," Perez told him. "If Manship did not control the legislature, what could the governor gain by coercing Manship?"

After requesting and being granted additional time, Perez took specific exception to the Manship charge, arguing that the information Long threatened to divulge about Douglas Manship's treatment in a mental institution was public knowledge. "There is nothing secretive about the names of persons being in the insane hospitals, although it is sad that they are insane." He pointed out that according to law these institutions provided the names of patients to the legislature. "I submit, gentlemen," Perez concluded, after almost an hour and a half of argument, "there is nothing that could have been coerced or that could have been contended to be coerced from Manship by the governor."

The vote was a blow to the impeachers. Twenty-one senators voted to sustain the demurrer, i.e., to dismiss the charge, and only eighteen voted against sustaining it. The Long forces secretly rejoiced, because they had in their possession the Round Robin that would prevent any further charges from being brought.

When the Senate went into session the next morning, May 16, a Long supporter, Philip Gilbert, stood up and said, "Mr. Chief Justice, on behalf of myself and fourteen other senators, I desire at this time to file a motion and ask the secretary to read it." The names of the senators who had agreed to vote against impeachment regardless of further evidence introduced against the governor were then read. The impeachers were stunned; Huey and his supporters had won.

The Round Robin became notorious in Louisiana politics, and several people later claimed credit for the idea. Years later, Perez told T. Harry Williams, "I couldn't honestly say whether it was me or Huey. We were talking one day, and the idea came to one of us."

Perez backed Huey because he recognized ability, and judged that Long would be a major power in the state. The Twenty-fifth Judicial District continued to give Huey overwhelming majorities in subsequent elections, but the impeachment proceedings marked the high point of Perez's direct involvement in the Long organization. He returned to Plaquemines to consolidate his own power—considerably enhanced by a friendly governor who controlled such appointments as levee board members, with their extensive jurisdiction over public lands. Perez had little enthusiasm for Long's welfare programs; more important, oil and sulphur had been discovered in Plaquemines, and Perez foresaw his own profitable alliances with mineral developers, and an advantage in minimizing state supervision of that development. By the time Huey became a nationally recognized figure and an advocate of sharing the national wealth, Perez was out of the picture. The scandals that followed Huey's assassination in 1935 and led to prison terms for Long supporters never harmed Judge Perez.

Brass Bands and Little Balls

Perez learned early to pay close attention to detail, and to involve himself personally in every aspect of the political process and the function of local government—including the disposition of public land. He perfected what was known as the "caucus race," held before each parish election. In the old New Orleans *Item* David Baldwin quoted an anonymous participant in the early caucus races in Plaquemines, admittedly anti-Perez: "A meeting is called and all Perez' followers are invited to attend. There is usually a brass band, beer, barbecue and likker. Perez acts as toastmaster, and most of the time a speaker is invited to explain how democratically things function in Plaquemines. . . . Each ward meets separately with Perez as chairman of the ward caucus. These wards select two delegates to meet in the main caucus, where Perez again sits as chairman. Perez makes all the speeches, and the procedure is to have an informal discussion of all candidates so Perez can cue the boys on who he wants to run. Nominations are always unanimous."

After a full ticket was endorsed, a second or "scrub" ticket was chosen, because that would assure a majority of Perez election commissioners, who were a big help in winning elections. By law each candidate could submit a list of qualified voters he wanted for commissioners, who conducted the elections; these names were placed on a list and assigned numbers. Numbered balls were then placed in a shaker and taken out one by one, and the names corresponding to the numbers were the commissioners. If Perez had both a regular ticket and a scrub ticket, the chances of his commissioners being picked were doubled. To safeguard these odds, partisan deputies would crowd around the table where the selection of balls was taking place, and jostle the antis out of view. The names not chosen as commissioners were designated poll-watchers, and the pro-Perez watchers would automatically outnumber the antis. Poll-watchers had considerable influence on illiterate voters, and on those unused to the voting process or those easily intimidated. Opposition poll-watchers often failed to receive their commissions through the mail until after the election.

Government in Plaquemines during the first half of the twentieth century was still based on the ward system. The members of the governing body—the Police Jury—were elected from each of the parish's ten wards, and were paid for each day the Jury met. They had jurisdiction over road, drainage, irrigation, and sub-road districts, and were entrusted with the care of the courthouse at Pointe a la Hache, the jail, and other parish property. The sheriff, justices of the peace, constables, and other officials received wages directly from the Police Jury, which also had power to levy taxes and to borrow money to operate its various boards. As district attorney, Perez acted as adviser to the Police Jury, which was eventually made up entirely of men he had gotten elected.

The school boards in Plaquemines were also elected, and they also had extensive rights to public land, much of which would eventually be leased to oil companies for ridiculously low figures. The levee board's members were appointed by the governor, but Perez's ingenious constitutional amendment had enabled the Police Jury to assume the debts—or the assets—of the levee board.

By 1930 Perez was already using Huey Long's system of obtaining undated, signed resignations from appointed officials, in case he ever wanted them replaced. The grand juries were hand-picked, since Perez appointed the jury commissioners, who in turn selected the names placed on the venire lists. Perez was not only legal adviser to the Police Jury, but also to the grand jury and the levee and school boards.

Perez's control of elections was subtle yet thoroughgoing. Elections in every Louisiana parish proceeded according to rules laid down by the Democratic state Central Committee (Republicans represented only a fraction of the electorate, and anyone who wanted his vote to count voted in the Democratic primaries), and the district and parish committees. Perez joined the state Central Committee at the beginning of his political career, later controlling it and using it as a platform to attack his enemies—chiefly the federal government. He also, of course, belonged to—and dominated—the district and parish committees. The latter determined a candidate's qualifications; since Perez controlled the committee, he could see to it that an opposing candidate was disqualified on technicalities. Additionally, the parish committee often made it difficult for opposition candidates merely to find out the proper qualification fees, or to whom the fees should be paid. Antis might seek recourse in the courts, but since Perez headed the Plaquemines machine, the district judge was certain to be pro-Perez. The lawsuit would therefore have to be filed either in the court of appeals or in the state supreme court, both costly and time-consuming procedures—sometimes the election would be over before the case was heard. The fact that Perez had supporters on both these higher courts during most of his career was a further discouragement to his rivals.

In 1931 twenty-eight of these banded together to run against candidates backed by the Perez faction in Plaquemines. But they could not discover whether the parish Democratic committee had met to determine qualifications. Committee members wouldn't discuss the matter; no one seemed to know who the committee chairman was, including Perez, who was the committee's attorney as well as a member. By law the qualifications should have been posted in the courthouse, but none of the antis was able to find the notice, and therefore they couldn't file applications for candidacy.

Undoubtedly there were many people in Plaquemines who consistently voted for Perez and the candidates he favored; there is also considerable evidence of voting fraud. A common practice was "voting the lists." The day before the election the names of eligible voters would be copied in mixed order from the registration rolls; the next day those names were copied onto the poll voting list, indicating that those voters had appeared at the polls, and ballots were cast for them. A few ballots would be left unmarked, in case someone actually wanted to cast his own ballot. The system worked because a voter was not required by law to sign his name on the poll voting list. In the ballot box itself, a cardboard would be placed on top of the stuffed, or fraudulent, ballots, and any votes actually cast would fall on top of the cardboard. These could then easily be checked; any votes cast for opposition candidates could be changed or spoiled. If a particular ballot box was known to be irredeemable—if the commissioners hadn't been able to vote the list at a predominantly anti polling place, or if the Perez faction wanted to neutralize a particular polling place—a discreetly administered bottle of acid would ruin most of the ballots

Occasionally the election commissioners—the ones chosen by picking numbered balls out of a shaker—were less than circumspect. Often a whole precinct would vote in alphabetical order; one registration roll in Plaquemines contained the names of Clara Bow, Babe Ruth, Jack Dempsey, and Charlie Chaplin.

When Huey Long ran for the U.S. Senate in 1930, he received an overwhelming majority of votes in the Twenty-fifth Judicial District. St. Bernard had at the time only 2,454 registered voters, but the parish cast 3,979 votes for Huey and only 9 for his opponent. (The sheriff, Dr. L. A. Mereaux, who was Perez's ally and the boss of St. Bernard Parish, promised Long supporters, "We'll do better next time.") In the 1932 Senate contest between John Overton—the candidate of Huey and Perez—and Edwin S. Broussard, Broussard managed to win only in the southern French parishes, with the exception of Plaquemines and St. Bernard. But these two parishes went solidly for Overton. The election was contested, and Earl Long, Huey's estranged brother, testified that he saw Huey in New Orleans on election night going over the returns from these two parishes in his suite in the Roosevelt Hotel. Huey reportedly telephoned Sheriff Mereaux to find out exactly how many votes had been cast for Overton, and was told, "We are still voting." Huey then shouted at Mereaux, "We've already won. For God's sake, stop counting!"

Salvador Chiappetta, a resident of lower Plaquemines and a highway maintenance foreman, once griped to other highway workers and friends that Perez had used state highway commission labor to build a private road and a pond at Promised Land. He was fired, and couldn't get another job working the roads or the levees; he was hired briefly as a watchman on a school construction site, but fired before he could report to work the first day.

Chiappetta decided to vote against the ruling clique. He had never before voted, though he was white and old enough; he drove twenty-five miles to the Pointe a la Hache courthouse to register, but could not find the registrar of voters—or even a registrar's office. A persistent man, Chiappetta made the trip five more times, a total of three hundred miles driven in six months just to register, but could never locate the registrar (who often drove up and down the roads, registering people at random, though this was not the reason Chiappetta was unable to find him). Chiappetta also wrote a letter to the registrar stating that he wanted to vote and asking how to proceed, but received no reply.

Chiappetta hired a lawyer, who wrote to the Louisiana attorney general, and on his advice to Perez, asking when Chiappetta might register. When Perez didn't reply, Chiappetta wrote to the President of the United States, whose representative—the U.S. assistant attorney general—informed Chiappetta that registering was a local affair. And there the matter rested. The United States government was not yet ready to enforce the Constitution in an area as remote and intransigent as Plaquemines Parish, where all "local affairs" were the affairs of Judge Perez.

Candidates opposing Perez in Plaquemines were often sent phony qualification papers, which if submitted automatically disqualified them; actual qualification fees were not posted in the courthouse in plain view, as by law they should have been, and the submission of an inadequate fee by a prospective candidate was also grounds for disqualification. The New Orleans *Times-Picayune* commented on such practices in an editorial:

"Political dictatorship in Plaquemines has stained the parish and state records with far too many smelly incidents and unsavory chapters. . . . The political annals and court records of the parish are so smeared with performances like these that 'Plaquemines politics' has become a byword the state over."

The disqualification of antis in Plaquemines was so prevalent in the 1940's that Perez was forced to call special meetings of the Democratic committee to hear their protests, but not to qualify them. One case went to the state supreme court in time for twenty-two antis to be made bona fide candidates. A candidate for governor in that election called Perez's efforts "an attempt on the part of the Plaquemines Parish dictatorship to install a system which prevailed in Germany during World War I," and another anti said, "These attempts to remove opposition candidates are based on the belief of a decayed and dying machine that 'you don't have to worry about the opposition if you haven't got an opposition.'" All twenty-two opposition candidates in Plaquemines were defeated: the machine was not yet "decayed and dying."

Eventually, Perez's position became so unassailable that he could afford occasionally to be avuncular toward the opposition. He admitted that he "threw out twelve [anti] candidates, as our committee ruled their qualifications were not in order. Their lawyer—he was a decent young chap—said, 'Can't you let us have a couple of them?' I said I had no objection."

He gave his own version of how candidates were nominated: "Let me tell you about the real democracy we have here. . . . We write to about two hundred people in the parish to come and bring their friends, and we publish a notice in the paper. Sometimes about eight hundred people come. Then we break them into smaller meetings, and ward by ward they designate the candidates for office. Can you find anything more democratic? That word, 'democratic,' has been so much abused."

The antis charged that only friends of the ruling clique were invited to the caucuses. If it was learned that uninvited guests were planning to attend, the meeting would be switched

45

at the last moment to a location thirty miles away. But Perez denied that there were people excluded from the system: "There aren't even half a dozen who knock the administration. We could easily have them with us if we gave them political favors."

Charges of election fraud eventually brought action by the federal government. In the late 1940's agents of the Federal Bureau of Investigation looked into complaints of voting fraud in Plaquemines, and five election commissioners were convicted of fraud in federal court in New Orleans. Leniency was requested by the defense on the grounds that the defendants had no previous criminal records; the judge granted the request, but made the observation, "When you're on the right side down there, you're not likely to have a criminal record."

Perez explained the convictions in a typically offhand manner: "Some of these Plaquemines folks don't have any way of getting to the polls, so they used to ask their friends to cast their votes for them. That's all that happened."

When voting machines were finally installed in Plaquemines, Perez candidates still received large—though not quite so large—majorities. Secretary of State Wade Martin claims that Perez was happy to have the voting booths because the official election returns "made liars out of the newspapers," which had often charged election fraud. A reliable source in the parish claims that "on most of the voting machines you couldn't move the lever for the opposition candidates. If you called the observer into the booth to help, then he'd know which way you voted." As Earl Long once admitted, "If I have the right commissioners, I can make them [voting] machines play *Home Sweet Home*."

Chapter
Three

The
Caudillo

There is a principle of law that says there is a remedy for every wrong.

Leander Perez

Murder and Other Inconveniences

Prohibition served as a great impetus to an industry that had flourished in Plaquemines and St. Bernard since the time of Lafitte: smuggling. The law was both ignored and resented. In *Deep Delta Country*, Harnett Kane wrote, "The Deltas . . . could not understand [Prohibition]; as one put it, some of them regarded it as a crime directed at them, more or less personally." Breaking the law became a matter of honor, and a highly profitable pastime in the Twenty-fifth Judicial District, which was a natural conduit of foreign goods into the United States. It afforded good, secluded anchorage in a thousand different inlets that could not possibly all be patrolled by federal agents; the mouth of the Mississippi was easily accessible to Central America, Cuba, and the West Indies. Outsiders were drawn into Plaquemines in the early days of Prohibition by the availability of a locally made orange wine that was dry and could be quite strong; it was bootlegged outside the parish, and even carbonated and sold for champagne. Other outsiders visiting south of New Orleans represented importers with greater ambition and broader interests; they made contact in the Delta's equivalent of speakeasies with fishermen and trappers willing to hire out their "luggers" (boats) for a day and haul contraband ashore. Thousands of cases of liquor would be loaded aboard a "mother ship" somewhere outside the territorial United States; the ship would come within a few miles of

48

the river mouth, to be met by the small boats. Sometimes signals were given over the radio (both private and commercial) setting up the rendezvous, usually near the Breton or Chandeleur islands, just off the Gulf coast—earlier used by pirates for much the same sort of purpose. The contracted fishermen and trappers then "milked" the mother, stashed their cargo or immediately loaded it onto trucks bound for New Orleans. The liquor could be disguised, or hidden in passenger cars or oil trucks, but usually—and especially in big operations—it was transported at night by armed men willing to gamble for big profits.

Federal "dry" agents were only a secondary threat; what the smugglers were mainly armed against were hijackers, who understood the radio signals and the trade in general, and often posed as government inspectors. The guards riding the trucks were in the beginning the same hoods from Chicago or the East Coast who came down to make deals with the Delta boys, but gradually local talent took over. A certain romance attached to the liquor runners, for theirs was a dangerous and desperate job; some of them even wore silk shirts to advertise their vocation. Regular battles took place between the runners and the hijackers, and natives knew better than to go driving at night.

Early one spring morning in 1923, the St. Bernard sheriff, Albert Estopinal, received a tip that a convoy of trucks would be traveling up from the lakes near the Gulf, loaded with whiskey. Estopinal sent his deputies, one of them a relative, to intercept the convoy at the Violet Bridge, which traffic from the south had to cross. Exactly what Estopinal's men had in mind is difficult to determine. It was not unknown for law enforcement officials to receive payoffs for the right of passage, to actually provide safe conduct for illegal shipments, or to commandeer the shipment for their own purposes. There was also an occasional arrest. Two deputies concealed themselves beside the road; when the trucks arrived, the deputies stepped out and ordered the convoy to halt. Two men in the cab of the first truck—one armed with a shotgun—fired at close range, killing one deputy and wounding another. He fell in the road, and died after the trucks had run him over.

The bodies were discovered at dawn; news of the killings spread, and armed men began to gather outside the St. Bernard courthouse. The incident aroused strong partisan feelings because the principals—the liquor runners and the dead men— were all local, and certain families were known to have a big interest in smuggling. Sheriff Estopinal traced the shipment of liquor up from the Gulf through a particular canal, and arrested a man named Thomas Favalora, who was suspected of being one link in the smuggling chain. Favalora refused to talk at first. He was caught between two equally determined forces; when the St. Bernard courthouse crowd began to talk about lynching him, he decided to cooperate.

Several men were implicated in the killings. One of these— an ex-Tulane football star, a wartime aviator, and secretary of the Lake Bourne levee board—was Claude Mereaux, the brother of Dr. L. A. Mereaux, who would eventually be sheriff of St. Bernard and who was already a strong political ally of Leander Perez. The other men were indicted by the grand jury, Claude Mereaux as an accessory after the fact. Within days Mereaux disappeared, leaving word that he had gone "to Europe."

A trial was held, and evidence was introduced showing that a employee of Mereaux's, acting on his orders, had ferried an ex-prizefighter named Gus Tomes across the Mississippi a few hours after the shooting. Tomes was tried and found guilty, and eventually went to the state penitentiary, but the others implicated went free.

Shortly after the trial, Claude Mereaux returned to St. Bernard accompanied by an attorney. He surrendered to the deputy sheriff, posted bond, and was released. Perez as district judge had all charges against Mereaux quashed. When District Attorney Livaudais attempted to get Perez to call a special session of the grand jury, Perez refused. In the subsequent impeachment proceedings against Perez, Livaudais and the other antis attempted to show that Perez had shielded the

Mereaux family. Livaudais told the court that he had visited the home of Oliver Livaudais, his half-brother and Perez's friend, shortly after the Violet Bridge murders, and had found Oliver and Perez in conversation. "Oliver . . . told me within hearing of Judge Perez," Livaudais said, "that they were worried to death because they believed that Tom Favalora had confessed and in his confession had said that Claude Mereaux had killed one of the deputies at Violet and that Gus Tomes . . . had killed the other." Livaudais added that Perez asked him whether Favalora had really confessed, and what was the best thing for the Mereaux family to do. But Perez was not impeached, and Claude Mereaux not only was never brought to trial but eventually became district judge on the Perez ticket.

The most determined resistance to Perez's steady accumulation of power came from across the parish line, in St. Bernard. Plaquemines's eastern neighbor also served as the setting for a controversy over trapping rights that threatened Perez's life, and brought him one of his few minor defeats. The trapping of fur-bearing animals became a big business in southern Louisiana after the turn of the century, when sources in the northern part of the continent were becoming depleted as American women began to share the European fondness for mink, otter, marten, and raccoon. All of these animals lived in the Delta regions, but the most prevalent animal was the muskrat; it provided a cheaper pelt that could be arranged according to color, called a different name, and sold at a popular price. The price of muskrat rose several hundred per cent in a few years, and made trapping—previously a difficult, exacting, and largely unrewarding occupation—highly profitable.

The fur boom also brought complications into the lives of the people who lived along the bayous and canals of St. Bernard and Plaquemines in relatively uneventful poverty. Most of the poor farmers and fishermen who turned trapper remained poor. Prices of supplies rose, local gambling houses grew up along with local bosses, and, worst of all, politicians began making claims on the marshland that had always been considered common domain. In fact, under the Swamp Act of 1850 title to much of Louisiana's marshland had been given by the U.S. government to the state, which had assigned the lands to private individuals; when these failed to pay taxes, the lands were returned to the state and assigned to various public boards. No one really cared who owned the marsh, until it became valuable.

Various officials and their representative land companies posted the marshlands, and attempted to get local trappers to work for them. The interlopers and their trespassing signs were greatly resented in both parishes, and particularly in the Spanish settlement on Delacroix island—an isolated, inbred community along Bayou Terre aux Boeufs in St. Bernard, the area richest in muskrat. The Isleños fought with the company guards, and then with federal agents; they lost every court case, but continued to resist the companies' take-over, threatening their representatives and destroying the settlements of the scabs brought in to trap in their marshland.

Finally a Trappers' Association was formed, itself a remarkable development among people as diverse and as independent as those of the Delta. Perez was one public official who backed the association and its claim to 100,000 acres of marsh, which was agreed to by the state. Perez even agreed to act as the association's attorney, and promptly sold the rights to the land to a trustee acting for unnamed persons. The trapping fees were tripled. Perez refused to identify the purchasers; the president of the association filed suit to have the sale rescinded, and the matter went to court, where the sale was nullified. Perez was accused of fraud, and threatened by several trappers, but no action was taken against him because the trappers thought they had retained their land.

Then the case went to the court of appeals, which reversed the lower court's decision and returned the land to the unnamed purchasers. The trappers removed all the postings on the marshland and set up their own guards; Perez and his associates arranged for the importation of a force of south Texans, including some ex-Rangers, to police the area and shoot any trespassers. That was too much for the Isleños, who decided to go for the man they considered responsible for the loss of their rights. An armed contingent marched into Plaquemines, and Perez narrowly escaped with his family in a rowboat across the Mississippi. He left his deputies behind to face the Isleños, who killed one deputy and wounded five others (they also shot up a boatload of Texan mercenaries advancing up their bayou), suffering only three casualties themselves.

Perez and his anonymous associates lost control of the land, but so did the trappers; trapping became an industry of monopoly holdings, and then the price of furs fell with the Depression and the flush times were over. Also finished were the times when there was not at least one active contender for every plot of land in the Twenty-fifth Judicial District.

The death of Sheriff Mereaux in 1938 vacated the top position in St. Bernard and ended that dynasty, though his brother Claude tried to assume parish leadership. Residents of St. Bernard describing themselves as "parish leaders" met at the courthouse, and it was decided that Claude would not accede to the position of eminence, but would retain his judgeship. The new sheriff would be the tough, savvy former deputy "Dutch" Rowley, and Claude would be assigned the secondary position of power.

Claude Mereaux owed much of his political standing, and the fact that he had avoided prosecution in the Violet Bridge murders, to Perez. The Plaquemines district attorney naturally assumed that Mereaux would cooperate with him, and was surprised when Mereaux asserted his independence by insisting that his nominee be appointed to a vacant position on the levee board. Perez then decided that Mereaux had to be dumped. He attacked Mereaux for politicking while a judge, and brought so much pressure against him that Mereaux resigned as head of the local Democratic executive committee. A Perez man was elected.

The overthrow move met opposition. Sheriff Rowley sided with Mereaux, and together they built up sentiment against

Perez. In the next election, Perez backed Manuel Molero for sheriff against Rowley. Perez received what he considered ammunition for an offensive when a dozen women from St. Bernard came to the district attorney's office with the complaint that gambling revenues in their parish were being used to buy votes. The charge was hardly a revelation, since slot machines were openly displayed in both parishes—in fruit markets, gas stations, barber shops, and even churches—and big casinos flourished in Arabi and other river towns in St. Bernard. The contingent of women accused Sheriff Rowley of "trying to bribe voters wholesale by daily handing out large sums of money furnished by the gambling institutions of the parish." Perez professed to be surprised at these complaints, and launched an investigation.

Rowley made the observation: "If gambling exists in St. Bernard and Plaquemines, it exists either with Perez's open connivance or open approval. It could not exist otherwise." In a confrontation between Rowley's deputies and Perez-Molero supporters in St. Bernard, pistols and blackjacks were drawn but not used; two Perez men were arrested and charged with carrying concealed weapons. When Perez heard about the arrest, he arranged to have himself and two sheriff's deputies sworn in as "special agents of the state police," which authorized them to carry arms into St. Bernard.

The Rowley-Mereaux faction was successful in the St. Bernard election. Perez's opponents were so heartened that they began another effort to oust him. Mereaux had learned a few things from Perez. He took the offensive, filing fourteen pages of charges including allegations that Perez controlled public officials in Plaquemines by holding their signed, undated resignations, and that he had attempted to initiate the same system in St. Bernard. He charged Perez with maintaining an "army" of deadheads on the public payroll, and called him "the direct and personal beneficiary" of Plaquemines's mineral wealth "through an interposed individual or corporation absolutely controlled if not absolutely owned by him." Perez, Mereaux

54

said, controlled public boards which leased land to individuals for "nominal sums," and these individuals or corporations "owned or controlled by Perez" in turn leased the land to oil companies. He charged that Perez and his intermediaries obtained "fabulous wealth" from royalties which should have gone to the public boards.

Other charges were that Perez had initiated a system of "deducts" requiring public employees to contribute a percentage of their salaries to the running of the political machine, and that Perez prepared "all minutes, contracts, instruments and other resolutions" for the various public boards in his own office, and then had them signed by the board members, who "in the main . . . are not even familiar with what these resolutions are and in a great many instances are not even permitted to read [them]."

Mereaux concluded his indictment with the allegation that Perez was "aping" Huey Long. "As a result of his activities in behalf of the Long organization, Perez has become the sole beneficiary of state patronage and boss of Plaquemines. He has boasted time and again of having been the author of many of the obnoxious dictatorial laws of the Long regime, particularly those building and cementing his dictatorial power in his own bailiwick."

The impeachment proceedings against Perez were eventually dropped, but by this time the antics in the Twenty-fifth Judicial District had attracted a wide and attentive audience. When the St. Bernard Democratic committee met and began making rare noises of opposition, twelve armed Perez supporters broke it up. Several of these were arrested, and their weapons turned over to the clerk of court to be held as evidence. The clerk of court was a Perez man; sometime between the arrests and the trial, the evidence disappeared.

In 1941, the registrar of voters in St. Bernard, Mrs. Camella Leclerc, offered revelations concerning voter registration to some newspaper reporters, after she was dropped from the Perez organization for failing to obey orders. Acting in sympathy with Mereaux, she said she had been fired for refusing to destroy records of fraudulent registration. "It's no secret that fraudulent registrations were in vogue. . . . People outside wouldn't believe the things they [Perez and his appointed registrar] did. . . . I acted strictly under orders of my superior at that time. I offer no apologies for the rotten system that was employed then. This [registration] book has approximately 700 names of fictitious characters which were protested by the Rowley administration. It was ordered destroyed by Leander H. Perez while I was deputy registrar and on my refusal to do so I was automatically removed. . . ." Reacting quickly, Perez filed suit for Mereaux's impeachment. A few months before the proceedings against Mereaux began, Perez's speedboat exploded. A friend of the Judge stepped into the twenty-four-foot craft docked near Promised Land, turned the ignition switch, and was blown into the Mississippi. Though he was unhurt, the boat was destroyed. Perez, at his other home in uptown New Orleans, intimated that his political enemies had attempted to assassinate him, though an investigation revealed that the blast could have been caused by vapors trapped in the engine.

The specific charges against Mereaux were that he had passed the hat among the owners of St. Bernard's gambling establishments and used the money to buy a new Lincoln, that he had written off an assortment of goods (pickled pigs' feet, cigars, sausage, whiskey, hams, rubber coats, boat paint, and rope) as grand and petit jury expenses, and that he had sentenced a man to thirty days imprisonment for poaching furs and then released him after realizing that the man was his hunting guide (Mereaux apparently hadn't recognized the man because he was clean-shaven). The strongest charge was that of operating a divorce mill in St. Bernard.

Mereaux was duly removed from office (though years later he was elected state representative from St. Bernard). Perez had won another victory, and Sheriff Rowley wasted no time in mending fences: he told Perez he was willing to bury the hatchet, "as long as you don't bury it in my head."

56

Just Folks

*We seek here [in Plaquemines Parish] to
continue the traditional American way of
life: freedom of enterprise, local control of
our destinies, high American standards of
living.*

Leander Perez

Perez commanded parish and family. After his father and
mother died, he regularly sent money—either his own or
checks from his brother, Michel—to a priest in Belle Chasse to
say masses for his parents. He occasionally sent money to a
poor and ailing brother, Olympe, living in New Orleans. His
own sons—Leander, Jr., known as "Lea," and Chalin—and his
two daughters grew up and eventually married into respectable New Orleans families. The Perez clan would gather on
weekends at Promised Land, and later at Perez's ranch on the
east bank of the Mississippi at Idlewild. The Plaquemines
Gazette, "the only newspaper dedicated to serving the best
interests of Plaquemines Parish" and by now exclusively Perez's organ, describes a typical scene in the Perez home: "Hap-
piness seemed to fill every seam in the house. It pervaded the
air. It was a bountiful home. Friends and relatives not only
enjoyed the hospitality in the home, but more often as not
when they were leaving, Mrs. Perez would fill their arms with
goodies—fresh vegetables, fresh fruit, preserves, cakes, candies
or maybe stuffed artichokes or home-made gumbo. . . . Because
of . . . the large number of energetic grandchildren, business
sessions that the 'Judge' carried on all the time, anytime, any-
where, were to the uninitiate at first disconcerting, but then
exciting. Here would sit this giant of a thinker, involved in
important parish business discussions while the little ones
would pounce up and down and over him, perhaps followed by
one of the dogs. The reaction? There wasn't any. This too was

part of his life. These were his children. He loved it. But then he loves all children. . . ."

Perez was known affectionately by members of the family as Lélé. He spent a great deal of time teaching his sons, and later his grandsons, to hunt and fish. He was an avid sportsman, and would invite friends, state politicos, oil executives, and even casual acquaintances to fish for tarpon at the mouth of the river, or to shoot ducks at one of the camps in the passes. He was meticulous in his selection of equipment, both for himself and for Lea and Chalin, much of which was ordered by mail. In the summer of 1945 Perez wrote to a gunsmith in New York, asking him to convert two German army rifles into sporting rifles, and to repair "a three barrel shot gun and rifle combination, being a double barrel shot gun with the third barrel under and between the double barrel, 30–40 caliber, made by the Krupp-Essen Works of Germany."

Perez never gave the impression that he aspired to any position other than that of parish leader, but he wanted that position thoroughly consolidated. (Robert Lobrano said years later, "The Judge told me he'd rather be a pimp in a nigger whore house than governor of the state of Louisiana.") He told associates that he was getting the parish "in order" so that his sons could assume power after him.

He most enjoyed being among familiar people, where he was "the supreme power," according to one associate. He always arrived late for meetings; when he entered the room, someone would say, "Here comes the Judge," and everyone would stand. On the hunting trips, Perez officiated. He did some of the cooking, making omelettes or oyster stew, and after supper organized rounds of bourée, a card game resembling poker or whist. He was an excellent player, but didn't like to lose. When he did win, he would sometimes return the money the next morning.

Perez eventually converted an old naval station near Southwest Pass into a kind of "boatel," and wealthy sportsmen and oil men came from all over the country to participate in the annual tarpon rodeo. Perez later air-conditioned the *Manta*, the motor launch that slept sixteen and officially belonged to the parish, though it was in fact Perez's private yacht and was referred to in the New Orleans newspapers as "Perez's Navy" (the single-engine plane and helicopter subsequently obtained by the parish were similarly known as Perez's Air Force). These gatherings and those at his private camp near Port Eads, where associates and members of the Police Jury went after meetings, were not raucous events. Liquor was plentiful, though Perez rarely drank, and when he did, took only a mixture of sweet and dry vermouth.

Perez's wife, "Mama" Perez, rarely went on these excursions. She was unassuming and interested primarily in domestic affairs—cooking, gardening, organizing bazaars, picnics, and parish functions, where she was often stationed behind the serving tables. She once said, "I always advise the young married girls to go everywhere with their husbands, when they are invited." She often accompanied the Judge to local functions such as speeches and ribbon-cuttings, but she disliked publicity and did not like to be photographed. She later became known as the "Parish Mother"—at least to the Plaquemines *Gazette*—because she organized Christmas and Easter parties for children on the east bank, and collected food and clothing for victims of various hurricanes. Mama Perez was also the only person who regularly exercised restraint upon the Judge. She often attended meetings on controversial subjects, sat in the back of the room, and gave a signal to Perez when she thought he was becoming too verbally abusive. She once prevented him from physically attacking a judge on the court of appeals; on one election day she wrenched the steering wheel from his hands as he was driving their Oldsmobile toward a political opponent.

Both the Judge and Mama Perez regularly attended mass, and contributed money to Catholic churches in Plaquemines and in St. Bernard. According to a close friend, Perez was not particularly religious; if a conflict arose between religious and political principles, religion came second or not at all. Perez's eventual battle with the Catholic hierarchy demonstrated this, and was a source of great concern and unhappiness for Mama Perez.

Perez chain-smoked cigars—at first Havanas, then, after the Cuban revolution, El Trelles. He bought expensive suits but wore them for years; he was rarely seen in public without a jacket and tie, unless he was dressed in hunting garb. He was basically frugal ("He'd put all the bread crumbs in those ome-lettes," says Dallas Picou, once a member of the school board. And, he adds, "Getting a cigar off of old Leander was next to impossible"), but indulged some relatively unusual tastes—he often ate rabbit, trout, or squirrel for breakfast.

Meetings of the Police Jury were conducted in the same imperial style as the hunting parties; they became social events where parish citizens gathered at the Pointe a la Hache court-house and listened for a couple of hours to Perez holding forth on any subject that interested him. The real parish business was conducted after the people had all gone home, when the jurors gathered for lunch at the only restaurant in town. First Perez would step into the kitchen and instruct the cook on how the chicken should be prepared; then preside over the details of every type of parish business, from the allocation of funds to the granting of commercial licenses to the determination of the size and shape of drainage ditches. (He once commanded a bulldozer operator to scrape off the curb of a state highway because the plans hadn't been cleared with him. The gutter was scraped.) He couldn't tolerate outside influence in the par-ish, and told an executive of a large national manufacturing firm who came to Plaquemines hoping to build a plant, "Sir, you are wasting your time. I don't want you down here. Now, with the Freeport crowd, we've got to know them and like having them around, but we don't want any more." He super-vised the filling of every parish job, even after the public pay-roll grew to include at least one member of almost every family in Plaquemines; loyalty was the prime consideration. He often received letters such as this: ". . . as for myself as court crier I want to retain my Job of which i have previously explained to you, as you know that I am still very active Prompt & dependable. . . . Remember that I have pride in the position I hold & its always with 100% Loyalty to my party."

Perez also expanded his influence outside the parish. In 1944, he wrote to Representative F. Edward Hébert, whose district included Plaquemines, St. Bernard, and a portion of New Orleans, and who was consistently pro-Perez, although not totally dependent upon Perez's backing to remain in office. The letter said, "Sorry I didn't get to see you after your strenuous campaign. Congratulations! . . . Keep up the good work, and watch out for extension of Lend-Lease after the war, continuation of business regimentation, and 'Uncle Delano's' National Socialistic Cradle-to-Grave plan." It was the beginning of a long and mutually beneficial relationship. Perez often looked after Hébert's interests in the state legislature; in June 1946, he wrote to Hébert, "As per your request, I have been trying to take care of Criminal Sheriff John Grosch in the Legislature and I can assure you he is very happy over results this far. . . . The Deputies' salary bill which I drew for Sheriff Grosch was favorably reported by the City Affairs Committee, unanimously. . . . I can tell you that Grosch is fully appreciative and he is just raring to go to work for you as soon as his legislative troubles are over."

Though Perez was opposed to Roosevelt's and later Truman's "socialistic" policies, he didn't break formally with the national Democratic party until 1948. As late as 1945 he wrote to the Women's Division of the Democratic National Committee an extraordinarily reasoned plea not to make a partisan issue out of the Bretton Woods and Dumbarton Oaks proposals: "Although a life-long Democrat, I cannot appreciate [these] proposals being sponsored as a party or factional matter. . . . To attempt to give [them] factional sponsorship can only tend to divide the American people." That same year he wrote to Drew Pearson, "I heard your Washington Merry-Go-Round Program . . . and it struck me as being the most sensible analyzation [sic] that I have heard with regard to the mistakes made by our State Department and others at the 'Frisco International Conference displaying the wrong attitudes towards Russia."

Perez at this time also enjoyed the benefits of having allies in the governor's office. Crooner Jimmie Davis, winner of the 1944 gubernatorial contest (he had written "You Are My Sunshine," which he enjoyed singing to the state legislature), was a lifelong Perez ally; he gladly administered increasing state revenues without causing factional strife. He was succeeded by Earl Long, Huey's brother, part of the old machine and a Perez man, until they split over the issue of the Dixiecrat movement and Perez became forever anti-Long. But as late as 1948 he could write Long asking for special appointments for friends, and get them; he also stipulated the men he wanted appointed by Long to the levee boards in Plaquemines, and once persuaded Long to call a special session of the legislature to appropriate $250,000 for levee construction in the home parish.

Chapter Four

The Miasma Spread

Democracy—I hate that word.

Leander Perez

Louisiana's Little War

In 1943, Perez established himself as the most outrageous public figure in Louisiana by bringing on an invasion of Plaquemines by the state Guard; it was also the first step in the extension of his notoriety to the rest of the country.

Louisiana's governor at that time was Sam Jones, a poor boy from rural Beauregard Parish and a World War I veteran dedicated to clean government and the eradication of the last of the Long faction. The scandals that followed the assassination of Huey were brought about by Long's political heirs, who, according to Allan Sindler, "inheriting Long's power and class support, solidified factional control by making peace with federal and state opposition, and then proceeded to conduct the affairs of government as a plunderbund."

The scandals involved government officials from Governor Richard Leche down to the lowest level, cost the state as much as $100,000,000, and produced a clamor for reform. Sam Jones, elected as the reformer, said in his inaugural address that he intended to destroy the state machine. "I propose to uproot it, rip it limb from limb, branch from trunk and leaf from twig. . . ." Perez of course belonged somewhere in that arboreal metaphor, being a Longite holdover (and one of the original "reformers") involved in questionable land dealings and politics that in style definitely belonged to the era of the Kingfish. When Governor Jones created a Crime Commission with

64

broad investigative powers and designated his attorney general, Eugene Stanley, to administer it, Perez was a natural target, though an elusive one.

Attorney General Stanley had taken a keen interest in the Perez-Mereaux battle, and had agreed to the grand jury's request that Perez be superseded as its adviser. Perez blasted that decision as "a piece of Mister Stanley's new democracy. An appointee of the attorney general can now replace the duly elected prosecuting officials of every parish in the state, regardless of how the people feel about it. . . ." After Mereaux's impeachment, Stanley sought to gain evidence that a monopoly of Plaquemines land leases had gone to a few companies, all represented by Perez. The commission issued a statement claiming that Perez "diverted to his own private gain, through subterfuge, all of the mineral wealth of the various public levee boards and school boards [and] corrupted the office of district attorney by setting himself up as a political tycoon and by the use of fraudulent registrations and poll taxes, had built up a dynasty saturated with crime and corruption."

The commission, using its powers of subpoena, ordered several land companies in Plaquemines to hand over their books for examination, and when refused, began contempt proceedings. Perez's old friend Robert Lobrano—then listed as secretary-treasurer of Delta Development and president of Louisiana Coastal—and C. P. Foret, Sr., secretary-treasurer of Suburban Coast Realty, announced that their companies had passed resolutions turning the books over to Perez and therefore did not have the records in their possession.

At an open hearing in the civil district court in New Orleans, the judge ordered Perez to hand over the books. Perez stood up and told the judge that the court did not have jurisdiction, adding that it was unconstitutional to issue writs of subpoena *duces tecum* for the production of records at an open hearing. Perez later filed writs with the state supreme court to stay the lower court's sustained order to produce the books, and continued to file suits ("Their number staggers the imagination," Stanley later admitted) while attempting to have the

Crime Commission dissolved. The commission was eventually declared unconstitutional on a budgetary technicality, and Perez never did produce the companies' books. But Perez's big battle with the reformers was yet to come.

The death of Plaquemines's sheriff, Louis Dauterive, in 1943 seemed to give Stanley and Governor Jones the opportunity they sought to unseat the Judge. According to Louisiana law, if a sheriff died with less than one year remaining in his term, the governor was to appoint his successor until the following election—the very same procedure by which Perez himself first became district judge. The sheriff was the second most powerful officeholder in Plaquemines; he also performed the duties of tax collector and had access to parish financial records. It was an office Perez could not afford to have occupied by an opponent.

Perez anticipated action by Jones and Stanley, and acted. Dauterive died early on the morning of June 1, and by that afternoon the Plaquemines coroner, Ben Slater—a Perez man— had been sworn in as sheriff by the court clerk and had posted a six thousand dollar bond under a constitutional provision that the coroner might take over the duties of the sheriff when the latter was incapacitated. Slater announced, "I am only complying with the constitution of the state, and Governor Jones is expected to comply with the constitution of the state."

Perez contended that Jones should call a special election because, he said, Dauterive had died with *exactly* one year left in office. Just in case the governor—who was absent from the state capital that day—disagreed with him, Perez had the courthouse at Pointe a la Hache surrounded by armed deputies to discourage anyone but Slater from trying to occupy the office of sheriff.

When Jones returned to Baton Rouge and learned of Perez's actions, he ordered the mobilization of two Louisiana state Guard units. Perez countered by ordering the erection of wooden barricades around his courthouse, and called a mass meeting "for the defense of the parish." He cited a wartime ordinance of 1941 empowering the parish governing body to call upon citizens for aid "in the preservation of the public peace, health and safety." He said Jones was "obsessed with the idea of conquered provinces to the extent of kidding himself into believing he could ignore the provisions of the state constitution and make a conquered province of Plaquemines Parish," and called upon "the hundreds of men—and I mean men who can stand and fight for their rights" to attend the meeting. (He told a reporter who asked when the meeting would take place that it was a "military secret.")

Attorney General Stanley made public a letter to Slater upholding his right to act as interim sheriff until an appointment was made by Jones (who was trying to find an anti in Plaquemines willing to take the job). Stanley pointed out that the earliest a new term could begin was May 19, 1944, less than a year away. The irony of the situation was that the jurisprudence set by the state supreme court in such appointments by the governor grew out of the case of Perez himself almost twenty-five years before, when he was appointed district judge; at that time Perez's enemies had attacked the appointment as unconstitutional for the same reasons Perez was now using, and had been defeated.

No mass meeting materialized at the courthouse, though a dozen vigilantes joined the deputies there. Cots and food— much of it prepared by Mama Perez—were provided for the defenders. Newspaper reporters who arrived on the scene were first told by Slater that the wooden barricades had been erected "to uphold the constitution." Slater then decided they were "for the benefit of painters." Perez told the reporters that "the sheriff question is settled as far as we're concerned." In Baton Rouge, four hundred state guardsmen, believing they had been mobilized to go into Plaquemines, arrived in buses, and were armed and drilled. Governor Jones announced that an assistant to the supervisor of public funds, a man named J. B. Lancaster, had been authorized to take over the tax-collecting functions in Plaquemines. Jones then went into closed conference with his troop commander, Brigadier General Thomas Porter, and other Guard officials.

Perez called a noon meeting of the Police Jury the next day, and by proclamation set up a "war-time emergency patrol" (the Allies were at that moment launching an assault on Italy's island defenses). The patrol was to include "all able-bodied men of Plaquemines," authorized to bear arms "concealed or openly" if the peace of the parish was "jeopardized by any unlawful attempt by the use of force from without, or from sabotage, or invasion, or imminent danger thereof." Police Jury proclamations also specifically named as members of the war-time emergency patrol all members of the Vidocovich Post Number 193 of the American Legion, whose commander promised to "back up anything that took place before the parish Police Jury." A warning from the head of the Louisiana Department of the American Legion, Commander J. Perry Cole, that the parish charter might be revoked was ignored. Cole, safely outside Plaquemines, made the astute suggestion to state officials "that we ignore anything they are doing down there until it is all over. Then if it looks bad, we might do something about it. . . ."

The *Times-Picayune*, the New Orleans morning newspaper, printed an editorial under the heading "Plaquemines War Dance" that read: ". . . Until recently Plaquemines displayed no exceptional consciousness of the war nor of the duties and obligations war imposes upon patriotic citizens. What has transformed her 'local government' heads almost over-night from somnolence and seeming indifference to martial fury so intense? Have Nazi U-boats sneaked into the river to menace Plaquemines' 'local government institutions'? Have enemy planes been spotted over [sic] Plaquemines' skies? Is the parish in imminent danger of invasion by enemy troops? . . . Does the custodian and commandant of Plaquemines' 'local government institutions' place more reliance upon armed force than in the law and the courts? . . . Whether the warlords of Plaquemines are resolved to fight to the death of their last openly or secretly armed patrolman . . . is not at present predictable. Time . . . will test their temper and should reveal their real purposes."

Governor Jones announced the appointment of Walter Blaize as interim sheriff of Plaquemines. Blaize was from Buras, in the southern part of the parish, the focal point of opposition to Perez over the years; a former member of the Police Jury, he was also a dedicated anti. He immediately filed suit in the Baton Rouge district court against the superintendent of public funds—a ploy to establish Jones's right of appointment—and mailed his oath and bond to the courthouse in Pointe a la Hache. Accompanied by his attorney, Richard Dowling—one of Perez's most persistent adversaries—Blaize drove down toward Plaquemines with the intention of occupying the sheriff's office. But just outside of Braithwaite, at the northern parish line, he and Dowling saw armed men wearing badges stop a car in front of them and question the passengers and driver. They turned back toward New Orleans.

"We were unarmed," Blaize later said in his defense, "and we didn't want to get into any trouble. So we didn't try to get through. . . . It's in the courts now and we intend to do it the legal way."

Perez denounced Blaize's commission as illegal, and vowed that he wouldn't be "allowed to take or hold the office of sheriff." He began a legal assault that was to become extremely complicated. First he attempted to file suit in Baton Rouge district court on behalf of Wilson L. Dauterive, the Plaquemines deputy tax collector and nephew of the dead sheriff, claiming that Dauterive had never given the parish tax records to the superintendent of public funds, and that therefore Blaize's demand for these records could not possibly be fulfilled. "It would be a mockery," Perez told the court, "for the judge to order the collector of revenue and the superintendent of public funds to turn over the records when they do not have the records." The judge disagreed, saying that the original terms of the suit must be accepted, but he granted a delay out of "an abundance of caution."

A defection within the Perez ranks gave temporary encouragement to the reformers. Governor Jones received a letter—which he made public—from Wilson Dauterive in which the tax collector asked Jones to make him sheriff of Plaquemines "so peace and quiet might again reign in our parish." Dauterive, hoping to accommodate both sides and profit politically, explicitly recognized Jones's right of appointment. Publication of the letter finished Dauterive in Plaquemines politics, though he denied any knowledge of the letter with the lame disclaimer, "I heard of a movement in Baton Rouge by some friends of mine to have the Governor appoint me sheriff. That was all before the lambasting started."

Dauterive dutifully resigned, with Perez maintaining that the office of deputy tax collector had also become vacant on the death of the sheriff. Perez issued a statement reassuring the people of Plaquemines and "our friends throughout the state of Louisiana" that the forces inside Plaquemines were united. Slater added that the "organization prides itself on sticking together," and that Dauterive's letter "upset us and was not in keeping with the organization's actions."

The district judge in the Twenty-fifth was now a Perez man, Albert Estopinal, Jr.; he willingly issued a decree to Slater prohibiting officials of the state Guard and the state police from attempting to install Blaize as sheriff. He also required Blaize to appear before him and show why an injunction shouldn't be issued against him. Meanwhile, Blaize's suit in Baton Rouge went before the supreme court, which upheld his appointment by a four-to-three ruling. In an extraordinary dissenting opinion, Justice John B. Fournet, a Perez crony, said, "Even if Blaize, armed with this decision by the court, seeks to oust the coroner, B. R. Slater . . . the coroner could not be compelled to respect the same any more than he could be compelled to respect the order of the Zulu king. . . ." Fournet added that the court in denying "interested parties" the right of appeal had "laid the groundwork for great confusion and disorder."

The *Times-Picayune* called Fournet's opinion "a strange judicial comment on the efficacy of adjudications by the state's highest tribunal. It appears to give aid and comfort to the

Plaquemines political warlord. . . . Enforcement of the established law is up to the state executive."

Perez was an easy and obvious target for the New Orleans newspapers, which could not be described as consistent champions of good government. Their editorials enraged Perez—this period marked the beginning of his hatred for the urban press —and he attacked them in turn. In a letter to the editor of the *Daily States*, Perez said, "I see you are up to your old trick of trying to influence the Courts by editorial. The same old hocus of 'TRIAL BY NEWSPAPER'. You pretend to be too slow thinking ('obtuse', it's called), to understand what I meant when I said that, 'Doctor Slater will remain the Acting Sheriff of this Parish for the full unexpired term of Sheriff Dauterive's vacancy'. . . . You know that your newspapers prevailed upon Governor Jones to appoint Walter Blaize regardless of the law, and the newspapers would not let him call a special election."

Blaize's attorney, Dowling, announced that "Sheriff Blaize will now go in and take his office, regardless of any opposition by force or otherwise." Perez warned that he would not surrender the office; the stage was set for an invasion of Plaquemines Parish. But Blaize again entered into conference with Governor Jones, and came out saying that he would not attempt to take over the sheriff's office immediately because the forces in Baton Rouge were "working on something else." He excused the delay by claiming that the supreme court decree wasn't effective for another fifteen days, an excuse Perez termed "bunk. . . . That kind of order . . . is effective immediately if it is effective at all."

Perez filed an application with the state supreme court seeking a new hearing on the original suit to determine Jones's right of appointment. For more than two months the court heard arguments for and against the hearing; during that time, the armed guard around the courthouse down in Plaquemines was maintained, and deputies closely patrolled the parish line. It was not until October—four months after Dauterive's death —that the court finally denied Perez's application. The *Times-*

Picayune rejoiced; referring to Perez as the "Plaquemines Schickelgruber," the newspaper said that Blaize's right to the sheriff's office "should be enforced without further delay." But Governor Jones continued to deny that the state Guard had been mobilized to invade Plaquemines, hoping that some settlement could be arranged. Richard Dowling, always pushing for a showdown, said, "It is now up to Governor Jones." Blaize announced that he would make a "friendly, peaceful demand" for the office in Pointe a la Hache with the backing of "a pretty big party," and what happened then was "in the lap of the gods."

On the night of October 5, ten covered trucks lined up at the Guard headquarters in Baton Rouge; they were loaded with guardsmen and driven to New Orleans. Eventually five companies—approximately five hundred men—camped on the bank of Lake Pontchartrain. They wore full battle dress, and drilled throughout the next few days. General Porter told reporters that his men were simply on a "training manoeuvre."

Blaize made a brief sortie into Plaquemines, accompanied by another dedicated anti, Ernest Hingle, and visited Slater's home in Belle Chasse, just over the parish line. He hoped to convince Slater to withdraw, but was informed that Slater had "gone fishing." Blaize said he would definitely go down to Pointe a la Hache the following day.

Perez filed suit in district court to prevent the state Guard from moving into Plaquemines. He convened the Police Jury and called a public meeting in Pointe a la Hache. The courthouse doors were locked, the armed guard there increased; persons not personally known to the defenders were turned away (a photographer from the New Orleans *Item* was encouraged to leave by a deputy firing a shot into the air). Deputies patrolling the parish line continued to stop cars and question the occupants. A deputy at the courthouse, Joe Cappiello, told a newspaper reporter, "They'll have to blow us off the map of Louisiana to get in here."

Perez obtained an order from Judge Estopinal calling the grand jury into session to investigate "complaints of alleged conspiracy to incite riot"—the charge leveled by the antis against Perez for his martial antics—and then personally took command of the forces around the courthouse. During the night, October 7, a delegation traveled up on Perez's orders from Pointe a la Hache to New Orleans, armed with an order signed by Estopinal restraining the Guard from entering Plaquemines. The men attempted to present the order to an officer at the encampment on Lake Pontchartrain, but were told that civil orders could not be served on military reservations. The delegation returned to Pointe a la Hache, from which issued Perez's further denunciation of the governor: "Sam Jones lied when he said he wasn't going to call out the State Guard, and you can say I called him a liar. . . . What do they think this is? Germany?"

The next morning Blaize sent a telegram to Jones saying he had "met with armed resistance [in Plaquemines]. . . . There is a condition of widespread lawlessness, insurrection, rioting and open rebellion." He formally requested assistance from the governor, who sent a telegram to Perez and one to Slater asking them to surrender the sheriff's office to "avoid the possibility of bloodshed."

Perez fired off his own telegram to the governor: "This is to advise you . . . that as district attorney and as an American and as a man," he would not comply with the order. He advised Jones that he and the Guard would be held responsible for any bloodshed.

In New Orleans, General Porter took the Guard on a one-hour maneuver through the city. He said he wanted his men to be familiar with the use of the trucks. Blaize was allowed to accompany the troops because, Porter said, he was "a friend of mine, and I wanted him to come along for the ride."

The road that followed the winding base of the levee along the east bank of the Mississippi down into Plaquemines was blocked in front of Promised Land; all traffic was forced to drive through Perez's backyard, where guards were posted. More cots were set up in the courthouse, farther down the road, and food was taken to the defenders by Mama Perez while they maintained their twenty-four-hour vigil. Perez continued to issue statements to the press blasting Jones's "military decrees," saying that the Guard was his "play-thing" and that the men were being taken away from their "war-time employment." He predicted that the mobilization—still not officially recognized by Jones—would cost the state a million dollars.

On the morning of October 9, 1943, Governor Jones declared martial law in Plaquemines Parish. He ordered the Guard to go in and suppress "insurrection and open rebellion" there, and to be on the alert for "threatened destruction of life and property." He added, "If one man or a group of men by sheer force of arrogance and contempt for law may successfully defy the entire state government and its highest court, then we have no valid government and the lives of all are in danger."

The Guard moved out at 7:00 A.M. in some thirty Army trucks, armed and wearing battle dress. The convoy, led by two armored cars mounted with .50 caliber machine guns, snaked south toward the Plaquemines line.

The vast majority of Plaquemines's residents had not responded to Perez's ardent call to arms. A few would turn out as spectators, but most of them holed up in their houses and fishing camps, hoping any bullets would miss them. The vigilantes, however, seemed more committed to the parish's defense than ever, and they swung into action at the news of the approaching Guard. Two long trailer trucks driven by blacks and hauling heavy drilling equipment were commandeered on the road in front of Promised Land, backed into the ditches on either side, and half overturned; left at right angles, they formed an effective barricade. Two dozen stalwarts armed with rifles and shotguns took up positions behind the trucks.

The convoy crossed the parish line at Braithwaite. Three Plaquemines deputies jumped out of their station wagon and bravely attempted to halt it by serving an officer with a restraining order. They were arrested and disarmed, and their car pressed into service. The convoy moved on. Half a mile above Promised Land, it halted again within sight of the barricade bristling with gun barrels. Porter ordered machine guns set up on the road; two squads of guardsmen spread out on each side, one cutting a path through the underbrush along the river bank, the other through a cornfield on the east side of the road. They were given time to get into position, then the two armored cars advanced.

What happened next is unclear. According to subsequent court testimony, a teen-age boy hunting rabbits in the underbrush and unaware of the invasion of his parish by the representative army of the United States, fired his shotgun. The Perez forces claimed that a guardsman fired. Whatever the truth, apparently a shot was fired, and it caused great agitation among the barricade's defenders. They discharged some of their own weapons into the air, and fled south toward Pointe a la Hache.

The trailer trucks were eventually pushed to the sides of the road, and the convoy moved after the defenders, who had time to erect a different sort of barricade. Just north of the parish seat, several truckloads of oyster shells had been dumped in the middle of the road; when the Guard moved into sight, the shells were saturated with diesel fuel and set afire. Guardsmen set to work with shovels and cleared a route for the trucks.

The courthouse was a scene of wild confusion. Perez, wearing hunting clothes and a pith helmet, loudly commanded a force that diminished in direct proportion to the Guard's proximity. He ordered all files taken out of the courthouse and loaded onto the ferry, which was to stand by with the engines running; a few curious spectators watched as filing cabinets, typewriters, and other office equipment, as well as a small arsenal of arms, were carried to the ferry landing. Perez attempted to rally his men. One deputy said he was willing to defy the Guard "weapon for weapon," but most of the courthouse guards believed that the Regular U.S. Army was invading, and decided not to resist. At the last moment Perez and his lieutenants boarded the ferry and escaped to the west bank of

75

the river, leaving Slater and a single fearless deputy sitting in the contested sheriff's office.

The guardsmen arrived, having taken six hours to complete a two-hour journey; they were met in front of the courthouse by Perez's nephew, Frank Giardino, who told Porter there were no armed men around, adding, "You can see that everything is quiet here." Troops surrounded the building, and the deputy —the same man who had said, "They'll have to blow us off the map"—made a final attempt to serve a restraining order before being arrested. Slater, sitting in his empty office, was told that Porter wanted to see him outside, and he told the officer, "Let him come see me. I have my civil rights." He was escorted outside, where Blaize attempted to shake his hand. Slater refused, telling Blaize, "You never made a fair demand for this office"—a point that became crucial in subsequent court proceedings. Blaize, staring at the gutted sheriff's office, said, "I guess I can file things in my pocket for a while."

Blaize appointed his own deputies, and had Slater's men put into the parish prison. (One said, "I give Blaize two weeks in office. Then he'll have to call the state Guard again.") The troops bivouacked in and around the courthouse; they set up their own kitchen, and began to search the town for insect repellent to combat the big swamp mosquitoes. Many local residents seemed amused by the invasion. The only resistance offered by the community consisted in disrupting calls to Baton Rouge by turning the cranks on their antiquated telephones.

Perez, meanwhile, sped north, in possession of those tax records that had not been dumped from the ferry into the river. He set up a government-in-exile in his New Orleans home, and plotted his next move. He issued a long statement branding the invasion "the greatest outrage ever perpetrated on the American people. . . . Jones is usurping the power of the president of the United States. . . . [he] finally summoned enough courage to carry out the New Orleans newspapers' demand to declare martial law and to send down to Plaquemines parish courthouse 1,000 members of the State Guard, transported in seventy or more U.S. Army trucks armed with machine guns and Army rifles with fixed bayonets in his futile attempt to take over. . . . As a subterfuge for his Hitler-like military order of aggression against the free people of Plaquemines parish, Gov. Jones and his quisling Walter Blaize [sent] a fake telegram saying that insurrection . . . prevailed. . . . Before Jones's State Guard convoy reached Pointe a la Hache . . . we concluded that to meet [it] with force could only result in killing large numbers of innocent members of the State Guard."

In Plaquemines, General Porter issued general orders to residents prohibiting the carrying of "firearms, ammunition or explosives," gatherings of three or more people, interference with military operations, and stealing. He added, "All persons who heretofore may have given aid to, or otherwise supported the lawlessness hitherto existing in this Military District, who shall immediately engage in peaceful occupations . . . holding no communication of any kind with any lawless person . . . will not be molested." His men discovered a cache of weapons— including a .45 caliber machine gun—hidden near the courthouse in a shack occupied by a seventy-year-old black man. Slater's men were released from jail; the guardsmen remained posted around the courthouse, and Porter said they would remain "until we reach the opinion that there is no longer the necessity."

Porter had difficulty in securing the use of the ferry, which had remained on the west bank after Perez's escape. He finally sent a squad of guardsmen across in a motor launch to order the captain to resume service. When the captain refused, a corporal fired a shot into the air, signaling for another contingent of men, who crossed and helped convince the captain to fulfill his duties. The courthouse was officially opened for business, though the machine guns remained stationed in and around it; within two days all but 125 guardsmen were pulled out of Pointe a la Hache. On the morning of October 12, in response to a rumor that Perez was moving down the road with his own troops to recapture the courthouse, Porter called out his men and set up machine guns on the highway; but the enemy did not appear. Mosquitoes blown up from the swamps were the guardsmen's chief antagonists.

Perez continued to denounce his enemies from his New Orleans stronghold. He protested the use of the ferry—"The State Guard has no right to interfere with traffic on the Mississippi" —and charged that the Guard "at point of guns ordered [Regular] draftees, including Pearl Harbor fathers, to stay out of the courthouse. . . . There are guns and bayonets and machine guns borrowed by the Governor from the U.S. Army in which our pre-Pearl Harbor father draftees soon will be fighting to preserve the American way of life and democracy and constitutional government against military dictatorship. Quite a travesty!"

Blaize, supported by fourteen deputies, prepared to collect taxes without the aid of the missing records. The state threatened legal action against those responsible for their disappearance; Perez claimed they were the property of the Police Jury and their whereabouts "the parish's business." Attorney General Stanley began an investigation. A vault discovered in a back room of the courthouse was opened by a locksmith and found to contain tax roll books, levee district records, assessment rolls, and file drawers from the tax collector's office. Also discovered was a record from the sheriff's office showing that a special consignment of weapons had recently been purchased that included a dozen hand grenades—none of which could be located.

Perez had apparently been badly shaken by the invasion, which he had never really believed the governor would order. But he quickly rallied, filing another petition with Judge Estopinal seeking to have the guardsmen removed, and going on statewide radio "to expose the unlawful action of Governor Sam Jones." On the air, Perez attacked Jones with the legal arguments he was to use over the next few months and which were to involve the state in seemingly endless litigation. "No state law," Perez told the people of Louisiana, "grants the governor the right to declare martial law under the guise of enforcing a supreme court order. The law says that such a judgment shall be turned over to the district court for enforcement."

The antis in Plaquemines took advantage of the occupation and began a concerted drive for local offices. Parish elections by now were only three months away; forty-five opposition candidates, including Meyer. Ernest Hingle, and Blaize, attempted to qualify. They went to the parish Democratic executive committee, but discovered that the chairman had mysteriously resigned, after announcing that qualification ended that midnight. The antis quickly sent their qualifying papers by registered mail to Perez. The *Times-Picayune* commented that Perez had in the past used the technique of having the Democratic executive committee chairman resign just before the filing deadline to block opposition candidates, and that by the time an appeal reached the courts in Baton Rouge, the election would be over.

Perez descended just over the parish line to Belle Chasse and met with the Democratic executive committee, disqualifying almost all the opposition candidates on technicalities varying from property ownership and failure to hold "true" citizenship to literacy. He charged that many of the oaths of declaration of candidacy were "improperly notarized," and said he intended "to file [them] with the proper authorities as evidence that the postal laws were violated."

Attorney General Stanley filed criminal charges against thirty-four Perez men for "lying in wait" and conspiracy to murder Blaize, General Porter, and state guardsmen. He also began ouster proceedings against Judge Estopinal and Perez, claiming that Estopinal had issued a court order containing false information, and that he and Perez were "liable for impeachment and removal from office . . . for high crimes and misdemeanors in office, incompetency, corruption, favoritism, oppression . . . and gross misconduct." He named in the conspiracy charges all members of the Police Jury who had voted a special $25,000 fund to finance "a condition of riot, rebellion and armed resistance" in Plaquemines. He quoted Perez as having said before the invasion, "You will find me out in front and not like a coward behind stone walls, and sending out men to look for trouble." Finally, Stanley sought prohibitionary writs to restrain Perez, Estopinal, and Slater from continuing litigation contesting Blaize's right to the sheriff's office.

The supreme court refused to grant the writs, a decision Perez heralded as a victory. He called Stanley's charges "a dirty political move on his part in an attempt to avoid his own trial by a jury in Plaquemines parish on charges of conspiracy." Perez hit back with his own brace of lawsuits. He named Jones and officers of the Guard as defendants in a libel suit filed in federal district court in New Orleans by the captain of the Plaquemines ferry, Elfay Galgout, who was asking ten thousand dollars in damages because the Guard had taken over his ferryboat and "threatened life, limb and liberty," subjecting him to "humiliation, mortification and degradation." Perez filed another suit in district court, turning the tables on the state and charging Jones, Stanley, Blaize, and Porter with attempted murder, conspiracy, and burglary.

Activity in the Twenty-fifth Judicial District court became pure burlesque, with both Blaize and Slater attempting to open court, in accordance with the sheriff's official duties. Estopinal tried to restrain Blaize from carrying out his duties, and the state supreme court was forced to suspend him and appoint an interim judge, while all litigation in Blaize's case was postponed.

Perez struck again in federal district court, filing suit on behalf of some Plaquemines deputies seeking damages for being arrested by the Guard. He held the usual quartet—Jones, Stanley, Blaize, and Porter—responsible, and for good measure threw in the former state superintendent of funds, who had initiated a tax audit in Plaquemines. Perez also blocked each successive move by Blaize and his attorneys, cutting off his access to parish funds so that he could not pay his deputies, charging him with kidnapping a Perez constable who was serving him with a court order (Blaize actually had arrested him). Blaize apparently operated in a vacuum in Plaquemines, without money and without much local support, often unable to find a justice of the peace willing to accept a charge without "an OK from Perez." There were in fact two sheriff's forces in operation, since Slater continued to pay his deputies with what he called a "loan" from the Police Jury. Blaize was protected by the order of martial law, but the number of guardsmen stationed in the parish dwindled quickly, and by winter less than a detachment remained.

A handful of opposition candidates, including Blaize, were finally qualified by the supreme court's ruling. Numerous suits and countersuits were pending in various courts throughout the state; the legal wrangling between Perez's and Jones's forces was complicated and almost totally ineffectual. Three days before Christmas, the judge who had been temporarily appointed to the district court in Plaquemines disqualified Blaize as sheriff after Perez demonstrated his failure to comply with several technicalities, including "an immediate amicable demand" to Slater to surrender the office during the invasion. Jones simply gave Blaize a second appointment, which was not energetically attacked by Perez because parish elections were only weeks away.

In the election, Slater defeated Blaize by a margin of four to one, and the Perez ticket was swept back into office. The antis protested that the election was illegal, that Perez election commissioners were illegally chosen, and that they had illegally assisted hundreds of voters. Their charges produced no tangible gains: they were still on the outside. Blaize's suit to obtain funds to pay himself and his deputies had not been heard by the time he was forced to relinquish the sheriff's office in the spring; the occupying force was reduced to an officer and four soldiers.

In April, the district court ruled that Jones's declaration of martial law was illegal—always Perez's contention—but the supreme court refused to review any more cases arising from the conflict. Early in May, Governor Jones revoked his order of martial law in Plaquemines, and the remaining guardsmen were withdrawn.

On May 20, 1944, Slater took over as the duly elected sheriff.

Dixiecraft

*We are awakening the people of every
state to the menace to the right of self-
government by the encroachment of the
national government.*

Leander Perez

Perez broke with the national Democratic party in 1948, and
never again supported the Democratic candidate for president. Civil liberties became the central issue for the Democrats
in 1948; resistance to the issue provided the basis for an alliance between the country's reactionary business interests and
the political leaders of the Southern states with the greatest
concentration of Negroes. The revolt had actually begun four
years before, when the Mississippi Democratic convention
placed uninstructed electors on the party ballot, hoping to set
an example for other Black Belt states so that they could seize
power in a close election. The move was defeated when the
legislature nominated another slate of electors pledged to
Roosevelt, who defeated the insurgents. But by 1948 Roosevelt
was dead, and the country seemed to be moving to the right.

The insurgents—nicknamed Dixiecrats—were to choose as
their leaders the governors of the two states with the highest
percentage of black people, J. Strom Thurmond of South Carolina and Fielding Wright of Mississippi, both ardent states'
righters. Ralph McGill has described the Dixiecrat movement
as "the most infamously hypocritical and intellectually dishonest political organization ever created. While it sought to
conceal its real motives with the cynical old shibboleth of
states' rights, its real principles were those later espoused and
practiced by the worst of the White Citizens Councils. Indeed,
many of the Dixiecrat leaders became the chief organizers and
supporters of these councils." Perez was one of the most emi-
nent. As always, he preferred to stay in the background, organizing, manipulating, providing support and often written

82

and spoken explanation of policy. He also looked after his own interests.

Early in the year, Perez's friend Fielding Wright in his inaugural address attacked Truman's Committee on Civil Rights, which had advocated an end to segregation and poll taxes and the enactment of a lasting Fair Employment Practices Act and an anti-lynching bill. Wright claimed such legislation "aimed to wreck the South and our institutions." It was necessary to break with the national Democrats, he said, because "vital principles and eternal truths transcend party lines."

Truman went on to ask Congress to act on his committee's recommendations. Wright then called a mass meeting in Jackson in early February 1948, and four thousand states' righters, including Perez, gathered to stomp, shout, and wave Confederate flags, while a band blared "Dixie." They resolved that Southerners knew best how to deal with their own problems, that outside interference was unwanted, and that "all true white Jeffersonian Democrats" should later assemble in the same city to lay the groundwork for a national conference of those opposed to presidential and vice-presidential candidates who favored civil rights legislation. The conference was to meet again in Birmingham after the national Democratic convention, to make its own nominations.

An early plank in the Dixiecrat platform was the resolution that efforts of the federal government to acquire title to tidelands oil violated states' rights. The legal title to offshore oil lands—the underwater plains of the continental shelf—and their leases had been a matter of contention for almost fifty years. The Department of the Interior had re-examined the practice of allowing states to have control in 1920; at that time the resources were already valued at sixty billion dollars. The federal government's contention that land under the territorial waters of the United States was part of the federal domain was contested, considered by the Supreme Court, and still undecided.

The oil industry, accustomed to dealing with individual states, feared that a switch to federal jurisdiction would mean

83

the loss of investments and existing leases as well as more realistic royalty terms, and so leaders in the industry began to warn against an assault by the federal government upon free enterprise and states' rights. Former Secretary of the Interior Harold Ickes accurately identified the real issue in the Dixiecrat movement, at least as far as Perez and some of his associates were concerned: "It's not a matter of states' rights, but the issue of the rights of certain oil companies to take oil from the states because it's easier. Those who are backing bills to continue state ownership are raising the cry of 'Stop the thief' in order to let the oil companies get away with murder."

Perez was a natural champion for the "tidelands" cause. He was a savvy constitutional lawyer; he fully understood the politics of oil and the benefits of oil production to local and state parties, candidates, and individuals. (For instance, Louisiana received for the years 1948 and 1949 twenty-four million dollars in rentals, bonuses, and leases from its offshore operations, much of that channeled up through Plaquemines Parish.) The term "tidelands" was actually incorrect. The land in question was not the area between the low and high tide marks, but the underwater land seaward from the low tide mark. States' righters claimed title to the three-mile limit, until it was discovered that rich oil deposits lay even farther out, and individual states began to claim "historic boundaries" decided before entry into the Union. Perez claimed a thirty-mile limit for Louisiana—a designation that came to be known as "Leander's Meander" (he later pushed it out to sixty-seven miles).

In 1945 President Truman declared the entire continental shelf a federal responsibility; the next year he vetoed a quitclaim bill, claiming that Congress should not decide a case still pending in the Supreme Court. Suits against individual oil companies and against individual states resulted in court rulings upholding federal jurisdiction, though Texas and Louisiana continued to lease lands beyond the three-mile limit until they were enjoined from doing so by the Supreme Court. Justice William O. Douglas stated for the majority that federal domain began at the low-water mark, and that "property rights

84

must then be subordinated to political rights as in substance to coalesce and unite in the national sovereign. Today the controversy is over oil. Tomorrow it may be over some other substance or mineral or perhaps the bed of the ocean itself."

The conflict provided Perez with his own special issue—the right of regional leaders to exploit the resources under their control; he found sympathetic companions among other Dixiecrat leaders. These included "Business Ben" Laney, the Dixiecrats' chairman and former governor of Arkansas, who came from a family with large oil-land holdings. Laney had been elected governor in 1944 with only 39 per cent of the total vote in a split among three candidates; his closest opponent declined for mysterious reasons to take part in the run-off election, and Laney became the chief executive by default. He ran on his record as a businessman, and conducted a campaign in which money was no problem. (A worker for Laney said that every bill for campaign expenses was taken directly to the campaign treasurer, who simply wrote out checks. He added, "Boy, that's the way to run a campaign.") Laney decided not to run again in 1948, so that he could devote all his energy to opposing the Democrats' civil rights plank. As chairman of the Dixiecrats, he proved fairly ineffective.

Other top Dixiecrats were Sidney W. Smyer, a lobbyist for the Associated Industries of Alabama; Frank Dixon, former governor of Alabama; Frank D. Upchurch, the old political foe of Claude Pepper, who led the conservative faction of Florida's Democratic executive committee in proposing that it and other Southern state committees block Truman's nomination; Roane Waring, Boss Crump's man from Tennessee who had put an anti-Truman resolution before that state's legislature (it was defeated); Herbert Holmes, chairman of the Mississippi Democratic executive committee; and Arthur L. Adams, chairman of the Arkansas Democratic committee.

At the second Jackson conference of "volunteer citizens," Strom Thurmond attacked the federal government: "All the laws of Washington, and all the bayonets of the Army cannot force the Negroes into their [white Southerners'] homes, their schools, their churches, and their places of recreation and amusement." The fact that Truman had never proposed these things in the first place was ignored. An effort was made to give the Southerners the appearance of loyal Democrats, and to make Northern Democrats look like the insurgents. Horace Wilkinson, a Birmingham attorney and an old Hoovercrat opposed to black people's even being permitted to vote, said, "There is no idea here of organization of a separate party. We've already got a party. . . . The idea is to coordinate activities of the Democratic party in each of the Southern states and in other states that will go along with us." The Democratic party in each state was called upon to select national convention delegates and presidential electors "who will publicly repudiate the President's so-called but misnamed civil rights program," and who would vote only for individuals supporting states' rights.

At the national Democratic convention in Philadelphia, this Southern intransigence galvanized Northern leaders. Hubert Humphrey advocated replacing the middle-of-the-road civil rights platform put forward by the platform committee— which the Dixiecrats had already rejected—with a firmer policy guaranteeing non-discrimination in voting and employment, and full civil rights. The Dixiecrats' reaction was by now predictable. The Mississippi delegation and half the Alabamans stalked out of the convention in what was supposed to be a display of Southern solidarity. Truman was nominated by a five-to-one margin over the candidate put forward by the remaining Southerners, Senator Richard Russell of Georgia; the battle was joined.

In July, the concerned white "volunteer citizens" convened in Birmingham, and after much oratory about invasion by black people of white homes, schools, and swimming pools, they nominated Thurmond and Wright. Contests shaped up in each Southern state between the Dixiecrats and the loyal Democrats supporting Truman. The revolt in Louisiana was led by Perez and John Barr, a conservative New Orleans businessman who was later to become a prominent figure in the (white) Citizens Councils. The Dixiecrats were equally opposed to Truman's economic policies, but this fact was obscured by the racial rhetoric which appealed to mostly lower-middle-class white audiences. Racist politics can produce unlikely alliances: in Louisiana, Perez and ex-Governor Sam Jones forgot their considerable differences and teamed up to help prevent the "black wave" that was supposedly threatening to break over the South.

Earl Long had denounced the party revolt in his gubernatorial campaign, but he sensed the general shift to the right and took a neutral stand on the Dixiecrat issue. The revolt was launched fairly late in Louisiana, but by August the fervor was so great that no prominent politician openly took a pro-Truman stand. Perez concentrated his efforts on the Democratic state Central Committee, where his power had been growing steadily over the preceding twenty years. He, Jones, and Barr persuaded the Committee to assign the Democratic state party emblem, the rooster, to the Dixiecrat slate. Louisiana Democrats had used the emblem on ballots since the end of the Civil War as a somewhat equivocal symbol of the fighting Confederacy (it was used in a dozen other states as well); the rooster had once been very influential in obtaining votes for the Democratic candidates, since it symbolized opposition to the Republicans of Reconstruction, and was easily recognized by illiterate voters. Although its influence had begun to diminish, the rooster was still believed to be worth approximately fifty thousand automatic votes.

Perez had a reason for waiting until August to launch the offensive. August 31 was the last day for qualifying presidential candidates and their electors: the Committee's premeditated action deprived the Truman-Barkley ticket of a place on the ballot. Perez's justification of this move was standard rhetoric for Dixiecrats throughout the South: "It is within the province and authority, and it is the duty, of the Democratic state Central Committee to nominate presidential electors for the Democratic party of Louisiana to support candidates for President and Vice President who will preserve the traditions

87

of the people of this state and protect their right of self-government and all other states' rights in accordance with our American way of constitutional government, as opposed to candidates for said offices who are pledged to support the enactment of federal laws to regiment our people, to destroy their rights of state government and to force upon them foreign ideologies such as the Russian 'all races law', here called F.E.P.C. [Fair Employment Practices Commission]."

Predictably, loud protests came from the loyal Democrats, from organized labor, and from newspapers in Baton Rouge and New Orleans. The greatest pressure fell upon Governor Long. He called a special session of the legislature in September and proposed a bill permitting the loyal Democrats, or a group of one hundred state voters, to nominate a slate of Truman electors on a "National Democratic" ticket.

Perez was outraged. He fought the bill through his own supporters in the legislature; the amended bill that finally passed allowed Truman's name on the ballot, but without the designation "Democratic." However, Russell Long, who was running for the Senate (and who had remained politically silent about the Dixiecrats), and congressional candidate E. E. Willis were allowed in the Truman column and the Democratic column, just to make sure their Republican opponents didn't get elected.

Perez contributed to the Dixiecrat campaign in other states, too. The presidential election in his own state was not really a hot issue; labor and black organizations worked quietly for Truman and Barkley, while Perez, Barr, Jones, and other Dixiecrats made all the noise. In October Thurmond wrote to Perez thanking him for the work he did in Louisiana, and in Texas, which Thurmond was sure would go Dixiecrat.

Texas didn't. And neither did all but four of the Deep South states, these being Louisiana, Mississippi, Alabama, and South Carolina. In Louisiana, the Thurmond-Wright ticket received 49.1 percent of the vote, Truman-Barkley 32.7 percent. The Dixiecrats' success was due in part to their securing the rooster for their ballot, and to the appeal to racial fears. Also, the

88

largesse of the oil companies was commonly thought to have played a considerable part in the revolt. V. O. Key wrote in *Southern Politics*, "The behind-the-scenes story of the Louisiana larceny has not been told, but rumors float around about tidelands oil." Perez denied the rumors. In a subsequent letter to Congressman Hébert he thanked him for sending him a copy of "Drew Pearson's unusually distorted statement regarding the 'Dixiecrats' and the oil lobby money, no part of which we have yet seen in support of the States' Rights movement."

The failure of the States' Rights party was a shock for many conservative Southerners: it marked a decline in the area's influence in national politics, and revealed a split between the middle and Deep South. It also made the conservatives, in many instances, more resolute and convinced that they were waging a kind of holy crusade. Perez's split with the Longs became irrevocable. Russell Long, Earl Long's nephew, later admitted that he had failed to oppose the Dixiecrats because he thought he would lose the general election. He called Perez "a delegate responsible for denying the people the right to vote for the Democratic nominee for President . . . a disservice to the Democratic party." (Plaquemines had always delivered overwhelming majorities to Long family candidates. In the next Senate election, when Russell Long received a majority in almost every Louisiana parish, Plaquemines delivered 93.7 percent of its vote to his opponent.) Earl Long compared Perez to a headhunter who was "still in the jungle and wants to stay where they eat berries and scratch for lice." Perez called Earl Long "that maniac in Baton Rouge," a reference to Long's temporary confinement in a Texas mental institution. In *Gothic Politics in the Deep South*, Robert Sherrill commented, "There were many Louisianans who would have agreed with both."

Perez continued to fight the states' battle for tidelands oil. He argued Louisiana's case before the Supreme Court, and based it upon a treaty of 1782 between England and the United States under which England recognized American sovereignty over lands occupied by the Thirteen Colonies and all islands in the Atlantic to a distance of twenty leagues (approximately sixty-seven miles) from shore. "Louisiana came into the Union with some rights," was one of his favorite assertions. He argued that the original coastline of Louisiana had been set in 1806, six years before the state was admitted to the Union, by an act of Congress which authorized and directed the Secretary of the Treasury to survey the coast territory west of the Mississippi river mouth, with special attention to the outlying lakes, bays, and sounds. That territory was later admitted as Louisiana. According to Perez, when the Enabling Act of 1811 was passed under President James Madison, Louisiana's boundary was fixed at three miles from the coast (i.e., three miles farther seaward from the sixty-seven mile limit), and not three miles from the shore.

"Efforts are being made by those high in the national administration," he told the Supreme Court, "to change the fundamental concept of our constitutional pattern, to adopt the European or Russian ideology that the national government instead of being a limited sovereign . . . is a government of unlimited power. . . . By this ruse the national administration is attempting to deprive the people of every state of property which they . . . own."

The New Orleans *Item* commented on this charge: "We get the impression that Perez contends that anyone who favors federal control of the tidelands has adopted a Russian ideology. . . . If that is true . . . the U.S. Supreme Court is just a plain old Communist cell" (i.e., by virtue of the Court's decision to uphold federal jurisdiction).

Perez's rhetoric tended to catch on among defenders of the states' rights to tidelands oil. Maryland's attorney general, Hall Hammond, who also happened to be the chairman of the Submerged Lands Committee of the National Association of Attorneys General, told the American Association of Port Authorities, "the doctrine laid down in these [Supreme Court] decisions finds its parallel in the writings of Marx and Lenin and the platforms and principles of the National Socialist Party, in all of which it is argued that property should be taken without compensation on the basis of 'need' for all of the people, regardless of the law of the land."

Perez continued to boost the cause of states' rights, and seemed convinced that the Dixiecrats would rise again if he and others set a good example for Southern politicians afraid to leave the Democratic party, whom he considered "gutless." He traveled to New York with Hébert to attack the Fair Employment Practices Act on a televised current affairs program; he urged the *States' Righter* upon all his friends and acquaintances. Secretary of State Martin wrote to him, "I am a proud subscriber—fully and officially paid up—of the *States' Righter*. Will your eloquent pen enliven its pages and enlighten our minds? Whether you know it or not, I am giving you a mighty big push in the 48 states through the Secretaries of State, the Insurance Commissioners and the top brass from every section of the country. You are known by general reputation and personal reference far and wide."

Perez was instrumental in organizing a National States' Rights Committee. An office was opened in Washington because, as he explained to a Texas friend, "it was essential to maintain an office in Washington so as to keep closer contact with developments there and to take appropriate stands against further regimentation or socialization by the national government." Perez believed the office did "a great deal of good in keeping alive the States' Rights movement and stiffening resistance of Southern members of Congress against several Fair Deal administration measures."

A committee meeting was held in New Orleans, attended by representatives from Alabama, Louisiana, Mississippi, and Texas. The representatives each pledged five thousand dollars to maintain the office in Washington; Perez personally put up five thousand for Louisiana (Texas and Alabama apparently never came through with their donations). Perez became the committee's director and opened a committee checking account in the National American Bank in New Orleans, and wrote the bank manager that he, Perez, alone would sign checks for withdrawal against the account. In 1950, writing to Frank Mayerhoff, a committee member in Jackson, Perez said that he believed if the Southern delegation in Congress would continue to go after civil rights advocates, the Truman administration would soon take notice and change their tactics. That same year he went to Dallas to address the States' Rights Democratic Organization of Texas; he warned them of Truman's "socialistic administration" and then gave the *States' Righter's* interpretation of various proposals by the Administration:

Even their false, misleading, so-called "free medicine plan" can't hide the socialistic grasping fangs reaching out to force all doctors, nurses, attendants, druggists, and all those engaged in health work, into involuntary servitude. . . . The Truman supported Brannan Socialistic Farm plan . . . is no different than the British, or the Russian, plan, for that matter, which is aimed at absolute control by the government. . . . The Full Employment Bill [is] another of those false and dishonest, misleading nick-names given to another part of the all-out socialistic plan. . . . The Truman administration would sound the death knell of free enterprise by another of its *must* bills called F.E.P.C.—more properly termed the Federal Employment Politburo Control. . . . [It is] taken right out of Joe Stalin's book and follows the line of Stalin's so-called "All Races" law in Russia. . . . Now, about Genocide. We find the Truman administration advocating a world government in which the U.S. would have a one-twenty-seventh part of the representation in an International Congress. We might as well have the Third Internationale of Joe Stalin. . . . a so-called Genocide Convention . . . is nothing more or less than an anti-lynching and anti-defamation international treaty which prohibits homicides, physical injury and mental harm against any persons of any race or religion or national origin. You will note the earmarks of the Truman so-called Civil Rights Program. . . . The Truman all-out socialistic plan would now be the law of the land. . . . In Louisiana last week the jovial Vice President made the astounding statement that "There is no turning back." How hopeless! How spineless! What terrible foreboding. . . . No, there is no turning back, there is no hope unless the people of the States exercise their right and sovereignty. . . . We have a heavy responsibility and a solemn duty to perform so that our birthright inherited from our founding fathers . . . may be handed down to our children and our children's children. The destiny of the people lies in our own hands.

Chapter Five

A Mighty Hunter Before the Lord

There are only two kinds of Negroes. The good ones are darkies, and the bad ones are niggers.

Leander Perez

Rumbles

The population of Plaquemines Parish was approximately one-third Negro or colored. The majority of the black people lived on the east bank of the Mississippi; a large and relatively exclusive mulatto community existed on the west bank, in the lower half of the parish, near Boothville, though people of mixed blood lived all over the parish. Isolation and a traditionally varied population had resulted in a great deal of racial mixing: it was not unusual for a white family to have a member with predominantly Negroid characteristics, and vice versa. And before the Second World War, nobody seemed to care much. Blacks and whites lived side by side on a totally non-segregated basis in many communities (Phoenix on the east bank was an example). Black and white children played together, often attended school together, and spent the night at one another's houses; their parents visited and ate together. A healthy naiveté existed in this sparsely settled and exotic land, where the living was easy if elemental, and there was little competition for jobs and status.

The *Louisiana Guidebook* produced in 1941 by the Works Progress Administration said that Buras, in lower Plaquemines Parish, was "the orange producing center of the State and ranks almost as high as a fishing and hunting center. Here people of French, Spanish, Slavonian, Dalmatian, Chinese, Filipino, and Negro descent make Buras an interesting miniature cosmopolitan melting pot. In the main, representatives of these varied extractions work side by side with little interracial antipathy."

The oil boom changed all that. Suddenly big money could be made by working the rigs or servicing them by boat; competition intensified the race issue, which was aggravated further by white workers from outside the parish who came down to work in the oil fields and brought their own, more virulent racism with them from other parts of the South. Black men who went away to war returned to find Plaquemines a changed parish, with white families moving out of their communities and old white friends pretending not to know them. The ugly practice of proving one's white birthright became *de rigeur* for voting, marriage, and good parish jobs. People had to account for generations of ancestors, and went to absurd lengths to prove that there was no "touch of the brush" in their family, all of which created a climate of uncertainty and misery and, eventually, violence.

Perez did not help the situation. His friends and members of his family claim that he did not hate blacks, that he did not even consider them inferior—just *different*, and basically incompatible with whites. His public statements, however, indicate that he did consider Negroes to be biologically inferior to Caucasians; the fact that he came to hate the idea of blacks—if he hadn't all along—cannot be denied. In later years he lumped Negritude, Jewishness, Communism (or any foreign "ideology") and the actions and representatives of the federal government into a kind of evil stew, ignoring all distinctions in the face of the threat to the status quo. Rumors abound—as they often do about prominent Southern figures—that there was Negro blood in the Perez family, that a close relative was banished from the parish because of his Negroid characteristics, that Perez's own baptismal notation was torn out of the church register. There is no proof of these allegations, and even if they were true, they would not explain his total resistance to the concept of civil rights. The Negro was the immediate, tangible symbol of federal intervention; Perez's resistance to desegregation was based more on economic than philosophical reasons. The probability is that he came to believe his own rhetoric, just as he apparently convinced himself that the Fourteenth Amendment had never actually been ratified.

Perez never had a particularly high opinion of Plaquemines's blacks. Very early, according to one source, he viewed them as uneducated and therefore as easy marks for exploitation in land leasing. But Perez supporters repeatedly claim that he was "good to Negroes." The favorite illustration of this claim is an incident that involved the draining of a pond on Perez's property that had been stocked with fish. Perez told blacks living in the neighborhood to bring washtubs and collect the fish after the pond was drained, "and don't miss a one." He then drove, followed by the blacks, to a nearby Negro church, and instructed the black pastor to hold a fish fry and "have a good time." The pastor complied.

Fielding Wright once wrote to Perez asking for tickets to the Sugar Bowl game for his black chauffeur, who had apparently told Wright that he had voted for the Dixiecrats. Perez sent him the tickets, and Wright wrote thanking him for his kindness in getting the Sugar Bowl tickets for his Dixiecrat "boot-black." Perez wrote back that as a States' Righter he was very glad to be able to contribute to the chauffeur's good time.

It was in the unlikely area of Louisiana's Twenty-fifth Judicial District that there occurred one of the earliest concerted drives to register black voters. Outside Plaquemines and St. Bernard, however, it received very little attention.

By 1952, according to the office of the Secretary of State, there were almost five thousand white voters registered in Plaquemines, and no blacks. St. Bernard had slightly more whites registered, and no blacks. An energetic young black attorney named Earl Amedee (he later became the first black assistant district attorney in New Orleans) and the black president of the New Orleans International Longshoremen's local, David Dennis, decided to conduct a voter registration drive in St. Bernard, whose black population was much smaller than that of Plaquemines. They believed that if black voters in the

Twenty-fifth District could be registered, then the rest of the state would follow. Dennis was a native of St. Bernard and felt morally obliged to attempt to vote there. He and Amedee did not know who the registrar of voters was, or the location of the registration office; they did know, according to Amedee, that if they launched a registration drive south of New Orleans, "the word was that we would both be floating down the Mississippi inside a concrete block."

Dennis was friendly with Representative Hébert, and helped turn out the black vote in the New Orleans ward included in Hébert's congressional district. Amedee described Dennis as "Hébert's nigger. Every powerful white man has his nigger. He loves him and treats him like a white man. Dennis decided to bargain with Hébert for the labor and black votes he controlled, and then get Hébert to bargain with Perez for us."

Dennis and Amedee flew to Washington together, where Hébert received them warmly. He listened to Dennis's proposal, and reportedly advised him and Amedee to go ahead with the organization of black voters in the two parishes while he talked to Perez. Dennis and Amedee returned home and began to hold what Amedee described as "vociferous" meetings in St. Bernard, at Chalmette and Mereauville, without interference from the sheriff or the district attorney's office. Then they staged a march on the St. Bernard courthouse; again there were no incidents. The woman registrar told Amedee "that she couldn't register those three hundred qualified citizens because Perez hadn't told her to." Amedee filed a registration suit with the clerk of court, and the marchers left the courthouse.

"I decided to wait for Perez's legal action," recalled Amedee, at the time a 31-year-old father of seven. "I knew that action would hit like wild-fire. That was before the days of Martin Luther King. People just weren't used to niggers behaving that way."

Within a week, Amedee said, he received a call from the district attorney's office, and was advised to instruct potential voters in the filling out of registration applications. He claims

99

that the parish had no application forms and had to print some for the occasion. ("Before, they just took voters' names straight from the registration book.") Within a month several hundred black people had filled out the new applications. Most of them were properly registered. Approximately fifty were registered as unaffiliated and another fifty as Republicans, and these could not vote in the decisive Democratic primaries. A few tried and were arrested, though never brought to court. "That was Perez's method," Amedee said. "He would file suit against an enemy and get him in a legal straitjacket, under bond, and then not do anything about the suit for years."

In St. Bernard, Amedee "could see Hébert's hand in what was happening. He was saying to Perez, 'Don't give these niggers anything, but let them do whatever they want that's strictly legal.' But the new word out was that we'd better not try to go into Plaquemines."

The office of the registrar of voters in Plaquemines was notorious for its transient nature. Often it would be the registrar's automobile; blacks coming to the Pointe a la Hache courthouse to register were sometimes told that the office was located on the ferry, which on such occasions might take a lengthy, unscheduled trip downriver. Occasionally the registrar's book could not be located because it had been left at, for instance, the Freeport Sulphur headquarters so that white employees could conveniently fill in their names.

Amedee filed a writ of mandamus at the courthouse, commanding public officials to act in behalf of unregistered voters. Perez had it dismissed on grounds that only registered voters could file suit. Amedee teamed up with another Plaquemines black man, a minister named Percy Griffin, who lived in Phoenix and had inherited land given to his grandfather when he became a freedman. He formed the Plaquemines Parish Civic and Political Organization to assist black people to register, with Amedee's legal aid. Amedee filed suit in federal district court in New Orleans on behalf of five Plaquemines petitioners against the registrar of voters, Frank Giardino. The morning of the day of the hearing, Perez, the sheriff, and the clerk of court went to the homes of the petitioners and registered them. Amedee promptly added the names of twenty-six black intervenors in the same suit. In federal district court, Perez appeared and asked Judge J. Skelly Wright to dismiss the suit. But Wright ordered the twenty-six intervenors and "all similarly situated" to be registered. Perez began a long tirade about Negroes not knowing how to register and vote properly, and Wright left the courtroom before he had finished. "Perez was left standing there," Amedee said, "with one hundred black people laughing at him."

Over the next year less than one hundred Plaquemines blacks were registered. "Some days we would bring fifty Negroes to the courthouse," Amedee remembered, "and Giardino would register only two or three. Perez introduced an understanding clause to the voter qualifications that included about twenty different cards. On each card were a dozen constitutional questions to be answered. Over a period of six months we didn't register a single black man. . . . We held big rallies in Boothville, we blasted Perez and the other parish officials over the loudspeaker. Perez's men would stop their cars on the highway and just sit listening."

Then the voter registration drive suffered a blow no one had foreseen. Griffin's wife, Irene, became involved in an unrelated argument with a teacher at the Devant school, walked into her class, and attacked her with a stick. The teacher wasn't seriously hurt, but Perez recognized an opportunity to strike at the Civic and Political Organization, and charged Irene Griffin with assault and disturbing the peace.

There was little doubt that she would go to jail. Perez communicated through an assistant to Amedee that he wanted to meet him at the courthouse on the day of the trial. Amedee remembered Perez "standing in the hall smoking a big cigar and talking to some white folks about his collection of tropical birds, and how he was raising seed to feed them. I decided to do a light Tom and see what he had to say."

Perez told Amedee that he wouldn't let Irene go to jail. "I'll get you later," he said. "But I'm going to give you this one."

In court, Irene Griffin was found guilty of disturbing the peace and sentenced to jail and fined fifty dollars, but the jail term was suspended. The courtroom was packed with black people; the judge called out to Percy Griffin, "You got the money?" Griffin said no, and the judge told him, "Well, you just bring it along to the courthouse when you get it."

Amedee said, "Black people had a shouting good time in Plaquemines that night. Perez even came down to a black bar in Phoenix and bought everybody a drink. But he was smart. . . . What he did was, he started a rumor that he had given me and Griffin $10,000, besides letting off Irene, to stop the registration drive. Griffin's men almost killed Griffin trying to get some of that money. They lost respect for him, and the movement died on the vine."

On other fronts, Perez continued his struggle for states' rights. He wanted Thurmond to head another third party effort in 1952, but Thurmond had learned his lesson and wasn't eager to repeat his Dixiecrat experience. He wrote to Perez suggesting that they let Governor Byrnes of South Carolina and Senator Russell "lead a third party movement as we did in 1948 if Truman or someone like him is nominated, or if the party platform is unsatisfactory. . . . The biggest danger that we are going to have to watch is to keep the people from losing interest in fighting Trumanism if Truman should not be nominated. I had rather see Truman nominated again because then we could have the direct fight and [I] feel confident we can beat him this time."

No strong states' righter stepped forward. Adlai Stevenson was nominated by the Democrats, which horrified Perez and drove him into the Republican camp—once an unthinkable situation. "Oh my God," Perez said. "Anybody who heard Adlai Stevenson make that speech in the Mormon Tabernacle. . . . Great Scott alive! I went all out against him, of course, and all of our people went along with us." He tried to push a resolution through the Democratic state Central Committee that would sanction a third-party voting device with which Democratic voters could stamp the ballots of Republican presidential electors, and Democratic congressional, state, and local candidates. When the attempt failed, Perez and his followers still rallied to Eisenhower, who was known to be sympathetic to the oil interests. Eisenhower made a campaign pledge to back a Submerged Lands Act recognizing the states' "historic boundaries." He kept that promise his first year in office, giving the state jurisdiction over three leagues of tidelands, a move *The New York Times* called "one of the greatest and surely the most unjustified give-away program in all the history of the United States." In the 1952 presidential election, Plaquemines Parish gave Eisenhower ninety-eight per cent of its vote—the highest percentage of any county in America—even though Louisiana as a whole was carried by Stevenson.

Locally, Perez was instrumental in the election as governor of Robert F. Kennon, a man partial to the oil industry who, after being elected, promptly reduced the gasoline tax by two cents a gallon, and added exemptions for individuals paying state income tax. Kennon's chief opponent in the race was Representative Hale Boggs. Perez attacked Boggs through a stand-in candidate, a long-time beneficial friend in Baton Rouge, Lucille May Grace, who had been registrar of the land office. Through her Perez accused Boggs of being a Communist, an allegation that, if true, would have prevented Boggs by Louisiana state law from running for governor. After Lucille May Grace made the accusation, Perez represented her in court, charging Boggs with "Communist activities" while he was a student at Tulane in the 1930's. Boggs denied the charge, but was forced into court to defend himself; many respected political figures testified in his behalf. Perez's "proof" of the charge of Boggs's Communism went as follows: "Alger Hiss denied having Communist connections. Congressman Boggs has denied Communist connections. Therefore, Congressman Boggs is as dangerous as Alger Hiss."

The charade was effective: by smearing Boggs, Perez brought at least some doubt to the minds of many voters, and Boggs was edged out of the first primary. Lucille May Grace's

chances were greatly reduced by the unfavorable publicity—
Perez was denounced in the state newspapers as "the poor
man's McCarthy" and as the captain of a "smelly scow armed
with mud guns"—and Perez quickly shifted his support to another candidate, before eventually backing Kennon.

Perez could feel comfortable about his national, state, and
local officials. But the Supreme Court was another matter.

Black Monday

In 1954 Perez was designated a "Doctor of Worldly Wisdom" by the Boswell Institute of Chicago, named after James
Boswell. This rare honor Perez shared with the unlikely figures
of Winston Churchill, Charles de Gaulle, and Harry Truman.
That Perez was also chosen as a Doctor of Worldly Wisdom
was associated with the fact that his friend from Lafayette,
Louisiana, Rousseau Van Voorhies, was chancellor of the Boswell Institute. In making the presentation, Van Voorhies described Perez as "the Leonardo da Vinci of the twentieth
century."

That same year Perez delivered an address to the New Orleans Young Men's Business Club on the subject "Racial Integration by Court Decree." In the address Perez denounced *An
American Dilemma*, the book written about America's race
problems by the Swedish sociologist Gunnar Myrdal. Perez
claimed that Myrdal's solution "was racial integration because
he held there is no such thing as race. . . . So, the highest court
of the land accepted as its modern authority for psychological
knowledge of the racial problem in this country, not the Constitution or laws or settled jurisprudence on the subject, but
the New York . . . N.A.A.C.P.'s hired social science consultant
and 'President' Alger Hiss's Carnegie Corporation Project for
racial integration in the South. . . . Intellectually and spiri-
tually there is no comparison between [Negroes and Cau-
casians]. Strictly speaking, the proper place to make the

comparison is in the jungles of Africa. The American Negro, by virtue of his short accidental sojourn in this country, has taken on a veneer of our way of life, but he is still rooted in the mores of his ancestors in the savage jungle life."

To prove the basic physical differences between blacks and whites, he listed fourteen indices found in a 1902 edition of the Encyclopaedia Britannica, including contrasting brain weight, cranial thickness, bone structure, complexion, and even skin structure (Negroes supposedly had a "thick epidermis, cool, soft, and velvety to the touch, mostly hairless, and emitting a peculiar rancid odour, compared . . . to that of the buck goat"). To prove his contention that the Negro reached an automatic hiatus in intellectual development at the age of puberty, he quoted a European who had lived in the South on plantations worked by slaves and who observed that "the Negro children were sharp, intelligent, and full of vivacity, but on approaching the adult period a gradual change set in. The intellect seemed to become clouded, animation giving place to a sort of lethargy, briskness yielding to indolence."

Perez went on to outline the method by which he thought the N.A.A.C.P. and the Supreme Court would bring about integration: "Beginning at the age of six, little white and Negro children—boys and girls—would be forced into continuous physical contact with each other in public schools and public school activities. They would study together, recite together, sing together, play together, sit together, talk together, and dance together. They would eat lunch together from food provided by the federal government. . . . The social theory behind this procedure is that this close and intimate association during the entire formative period of their lives would, in itself, produce integration or, in other words, amalgamation of the races. Fantastic as it may appear, the social aim is a Negroid South."

The reason for his attack upon the Supreme Court was its unanimous decision, offered by Chief Justice Earl Warren, that the history of the Fourteenth Amendment was "inconclusive" in regard to school desegregation, and that the "separate but equal" doctrine could no longer apply to the nation's public

105

schools. Within a year the court would order public schools to desegregate "with all deliberate speed." Two months after the decision—the day of its delivery became known among its opponents as "Black Monday"—segregationists and states' righters from eleven states met secretly in New Orleans and formed the white Citizens Councils of America.

The Citizens Council was, essentially, a kind of up-front, respectable organization for potential Ku Klux Klansmen. Louisiana already had a smaller anti-integration group, founded by a Baton Rouge contractor and called The Southern Gentlemen's Organization, dedicated to the defeat of "the Negroes' prime object—to marry white people." The first national chairman of the Citizens Councils was also from Louisiana, a state senator and Perez man from a northern parish named William ("Call Me Willie") Rainach. He also became chairman of the state legislature's Joint Committee on Segregation, which purged "irregularly registered" black voters from the rolls. Earl Long once claimed that Rainach, after delivering a tirade against Negroes, would "get up on his front porch, take off his shoes, wash his feet, look at the moon and get close to God." Other Citizens Council members were John Barr, an ardent Louisiana Dixiecrat; Tom Brady, a Mississippi circuit court judge, and author of the racist pamphlet *Black Monday*; Roy Harris, a Georgia lawyer who published the Augusta *Courier* and would organize the Democrats for Goldwater movement; and William Simmons, editor of *The Citizen*, and Richard Morphew, head of the Citizens Council Forum and the producer of radio and television programs opposing desegregation, both of Jackson. And of course Perez, an early organizer who preferred not to accept an official title.

The early Citizens Council meetings in New Orleans were dedicated to building up membership. Perez apparently believed that a concerted, large-scale resistance to desegregation in the South would discourage the federal government from implementing the Supreme Court orders. Citizens Council rhetoric was blatantly racist; in New Orleans, a considerable group of moderate whites remained silent. Newspaper reporters covering the Council meetings at the Municipal Auditorium felt uneasy and often afraid in the presence of hostile segregationists who frequently jammed the aisles, while Perez and others denounced their newspapers along with the Supreme Court, the N.A.A.C.P., and the Communists, and called for "mass action" to defeat desegregation.

During this period Perez met George Singelmann at a Council meeting. Singelmann worked in the make-up department of a local afternoon paper, and when the *States* and the *Item* merged and he found himself without a job, Perez hired him as a personal assistant. He became known as "Perez's satchel man," accompanying Perez almost everywhere he went, carrying his papers, making phone calls, running out of a meeting to buy cigars. Singelmann describes Perez as the "spearhead" for the Citizens Councils. "The Judge set up the mechanics for the Council in New Orleans and state-wide. He spoke all over the South. . . . We eventually built up the New Orleans membership to about 50,000. . . . The Judge knew Negroes were different physically from whites. He had experts in anthropology study the situation."

Perez had not yet advocated violence by whites against blacks in preventing integration, which he still thought could be done legislatively. He spent a lot of time in Baton Rouge, talking to state legislators and drawing up bills for them to introduce, and advising other segregationists throughout the South. According to Singelmann, "the phone rang all day long with segregationists calling. In the mornings we hit the sidewalk *going*, I guarantee you. The Judge knew everybody in the legislature, he wrote half the bills passed in Louisiana. He could write a bill any way they wanted. The Judge would write a bill and get somebody from north Louisiana to introduce it, if he didn't want the others to know whose bill it was. I'm telling you, we operated. It was hard, keeping an eye on all the Judge's legislators. He was an effective entertainer—he always invited a different one out to lunch."

Perez was indeed "the third house of the Louisiana legislature," and it was unthinkable to open a legislative session without the Judge being present. He would swagger around the floor and lounge in legislators' chairs while instructing them. He didn't hesitate to address the Speaker, though he was never an actual member of either house. He also frequently traveled to Washington for the cause of segregation and states' rights. "We'd go to Washington," says Singelmann, "like you'd go to lunch. Sometimes we'd fly out at 7 A.M., and be back by suppertime."

Early in 1956 Perez and his forces suffered a double setback. Archbishop Joseph Francis Rummel issued a pastoral letter to be read at all masses in the archdiocese of New Orleans, stating that "racial segregation is morally wrong and sinful," and announcing that desegregation would begin on a gradual basis in the parochial elementary schools of the archdiocese. And Federal District Court Judge J. Skelly Wright ordered the public schools in New Orleans desegregated.

Perez's reaction was quick and unequivocal. He accused the Catholic hierarchy of "turning against their own people" (when Rummel later suffered a fall and was confined to his bed, Perez intimated that he was being punished for his stand against segregation). St. Bernard Parish schools opened their doors to "refugees" from schools to be integrated in New Orleans, and Perez let it be known that no black child would ever enter a white school in Plaquemines.

Token desegregation was attained in New Orleans. Blacks were allowed into professional schools and the local branch of Louisiana State University; they were admitted on equal terms to parks, sporting events, even buses. The public schools, however, despite Judge Wright's order remained segregated.

In March 1957, Perez appeared before the Senate Judiciary Subcommittee to testify against civil rights legislation then before Congress. He attacked the bills as being part of a communist plot: "It is evident that this type of legislation is being considered for political expediency to mollify Communist-bent minority groups, principally the N.A.A.C.P." He added that one of the N.A.A.C.P.'s chief allies was Richard Nixon. In this type of presentation, he often quoted from a brochure put out by the Richmond Area Defenders which included Lincoln's address to a group of blacks on the White House lawn in 1862 ("Your race suffer very greatly, many of them, by living among us, while ours suffer from your presence. In a word, we suffer on each side. . . .."), and from Thomas Jefferson's speech about the threat of federal courts ("The great object of my fear is the Federal Judiciary. That body, like gravity, ever acting, with noiseless foot, and in alarming advance, gaining ground step by step, and holding what it gains, is engulfing insidiously the [state] governments into the jaws of that which feeds them."). The brochure also contained the notorious Communist threat to capitalist countries: "Speaking in Moscow thirty years ago, to the Lenin School of Political Warfare, at Moscow, the man who presided over the United Nations Security Council in 1949, Dimitry A. Manuilsky . . . said this: 'War to the hilt between Communism and Capitalism is inevitable. Today, of course, we are not strong enough to attack. Our time will come in thirty or forty years. To win we shall need the element of surprise. The bourgeoisie will have to be put to sleep. We shall begin by launching the most spectacular peace movement on record. There will be electrifying overtures and unheard-of concessions. The Capitalist countries, stupid and decadent, will rejoice to cooperate in their own destruction. They will leap at another chance to be friends. As soon as their guard is down, we shall smash them with our clenched fist.' "

That same year Perez wrote to Senator James O. Eastland of Mississippi, then chairman of the Internal Security Committee, suggesting that automatic "sanctions" be taken against any individual or organization suspected by the U.S. Attorney General of being controlled by the "Communist conspiracy." Eastland wrote a long letter back suggesting that such an action "might well result in the [Subversive Activities Control Act] being declared unconstitutional," a consequence which neither he nor Perez wanted. Eastland went on to deplore the adoption of a hearing procedure in connection with designating names to that list because "the process of naming an organization on that list took on the appearance of a semi-judicial determination, and it was inevitable from that point forward that there should be demands for additional procedure and assertions of alleged rights . . . which cannot be accorded without undermining the efficacy and reliability of the Justice Department's system of gathering information. I shall certainly give further thought to your suggestion, and I think you know how much I appreciate your continued and active interest in strengthening and encouraging opposition to Communism and all other forms of subversion."

A year later Perez sent Eastland a list of people and organizations in Louisiana which he considered to be subversive. He wrote, "I should appreciate whatever Communist-front and subversive information from the House Un-American Activities Committee or any other source on these parties which may be available." Perez also wrote to Secretary of State Martin asking for the latest membership list of the Louisiana chapter of the American Civil Liberties Union, the Southern Conference Educational Fund, and "if it is registered, the names of the Board of Directors and Members of the FOREIGN POLICY ASSOCIATION." And he wrote to Representative Edwin Willis of the House Un-American Activities Committee asking for bound volumes of the 1956 report on Communist political subversion, and any similar reports which "will be of great assistance in our checkup by the Louisiana Legislative Committee for investigation in subversive activities in Louisiana."

Perez could devote an increasing amount of time to segregationist activities because his sons, both lawyers, handled more and more of his private and public business. He was a frequent and often lavish contributor to segregationist organizations throughout the South, including the Citizens Council Forum, and could perform various duties for officials in Louisiana and in other states. Governor Faubus of Arkansas wrote Perez asking for information about a prominent doctor at New Orleans Charity Hospital. Perez wrote back that the doctor in question was from an old family and was a staunch segregationist and States' Righter.

In Louisiana's racist 1959 gubernatorial campaign, Perez

backed "Call Me Willie" Rainach, who placed third in the first primary, after Perez's enemy deLesseps Morrison and singer Jimmie Davis. At Perez's bidding, Rainach endorsed Davis in the second primary, forcing Davis to take a "tough" stand against civil rights and desegregation. Davis won the election, and assumed office in Baton Rouge by leading his horse, Sunshine, up the Capitol steps. Two of his activities as governor were to travel to Hollywood to make a film about himself, and to create authority for the construction of the notorious thirty-million-dollar Sunshine Bridge across the Mississippi River, which arched up out of one sugar cane field and down into another, and understandably failed to earn much revenue— except for those who built it.

In Plaquemines, Perez and the Police Jury appropriated fifteen thousand dollars of the taxpayers' money to investigate the "doubtful origin" of the Fourteenth Amendment. Perez claimed that it was "ratified at a time when there was carpet-bagger rule in the South and a great many people were disenfranchised. We had a Negro senator in Plaquemines then, and there were others all over the South. Through their efforts and the coercion of federal troops the Amendment was ratified."

School desegregation deadlines set in New Orleans by Judge Wright and Archbishop Rummel came and went. Opposition in the state was strong enough to unite the traditionally inimical north Louisiana hill country, cosmopolitan New Orleans, and Catholic country parishes. When Judge Wright set another deadline, March 1, 1960, it too passed without action by school authorities. Governor Davis had announced that he would go to jail rather than allow Louisiana schools to be integrated. At this time Martin Luther King was leading demonstrations in Montgomery, and various national civil rights leaders had telegraphed President Eisenhower asking for federal protection for the demonstrators. Perez sent Eisenhower a voluminous telegram attacking Walter Reuther, Roy Wilkins, and King, and asked, "Mr. President, do you realize that Communist fronts have made such inroads in our national government that members of Communist front organizations actually sit in Congress and are the loudest in their support for anti-South so-called civil rights legislation? . . . Halt Communist influence in our national affairs before this country suffers the same fate as has befallen several others due to Communist influence in their government. Mr. President, please let us not be beguiled and say, 'It can't happen here.' "

In New Orleans, Judge Wright announced his own plan for desegregation: it would begin in September in the first grade, and would continue with the desegregation of an additional class each year. Wright suffered ostracism among his social peers in the city, and a cross was burned on his lawn. Perez attacked Wright and Judge Herbert Christenberry. He told a crowd in the Chalmette courthouse—many of its members residents of New Orleans—that the American way of life was being subverted by "Zionist Jews," and that "courage is the only answer to the crisis we face. . . . We can't afford to keep running away from the Negroes. . . . There is a certain class of people in New Orleans today who are licking their chops at this situation. They are the most dangerous people in this country today—the Zionist Jews. You have no idea of the influence and the campaign they are conducting to raise funds to see this thing [integration] through. They are the backers of Save Our Schools, the Committee on Public Education, the Anti-Defamation League and the N.A.A.C.P." To loud applause and hog-calling, Perez traced the history of the N.A.A.C.P., "a Communist front organization founded in 1909," and compared its aims with those of the Communists and the national Democrats. "This is the Communist cold war now being carried out by politicians on the national level. The only answer is white solidarity, and courage. Nobody is going to save you. You have to do it yourself."

Perez spent the months before the desegregation deadline in Baton Rouge, after ordering the closing to blacks of library services in Plaquemines and the removal of all books mentioning the United Nations (supposedly a nest of "Zionists") or published by UNESCO, "showing a liberal viewpoint," or speaking favorably of the Negro race. "Wipe that filth from the shelves," he commanded. In the capital he set up operations in his hotel room and in the office of Secretary of State Martin. Perez didn't bother to disguise the fact that he was largely the author of an unbroken flow of anti-desegregation bills, many of which were adopted (only to be struck down by the courts) at a cost of more than $700,000 to Louisiana taxpayers. The bills themselves could do nothing but delay desegregation. One act gave Governor Davis the power to take over the New Orleans schools, automatically superseding the city's school board, which had already decided to desegregate. Judge Wright and two other federal judges declared the move illegal, but a two-month delay was obtained. November 14, 1960, was the final date set for desegregation to begin, and four black girls were chosen to be enrolled in the first grades of two previously all-white schools.

Segregationist reaction was frenzied. At a meeting of the Citizens Council in New Orleans, a group of white children—half of them wearing blackface—performed a skit that was to demonstrate the "perils of the future" in which they pretended to kiss and hug with abandon. At yet another session of the legislature in Baton Rouge, the august Louisiana lawmakers declared November 14 a state holiday. They ignored restraining orders issued by Judge Wright, and sent state troopers in plainclothes to each New Orleans public school demanding that the schools be closed—demands that the school board ignored.

On the morning of November 14, there were no crowds around the schools to be desegregated, the William Frantz School and McDonogh No. 19, because their names had been withheld by the board. But large numbers of policemen stationed outside the schools quickly drew attention to them. Approximately one-quarter of the pupils at each school showed up, and less than half of those remained for afternoon classes. The following day, only forty-five students attended Frantz, and only twenty, McDonogh. Mothers stalked into the classrooms and removed their children's belongings, saying they would not return while Negro children were in the school.

Outside, angry whites crowded the school entrances, scream-
ing insults at the black children and their parents, while cars
draped with Rebel flags drove up and down the streets.

More than five thousand segregationists attended a mass
meeting at the Municipal Auditorium, where they whooped
and stomped when told by state representative John Garrett,
chairman of the Joint Legislative Committee on Segregation,
that they were faced with "total war" and must use "every
weapon at [their] command." Perez stood up and told the
gathering in unequivocal terms that desegregation was part of
the Communist plot backed by the N.A.A.C.P. and the "Zionist
Jews," and that they must act. "Don't wait for your daughters
to be raped by these Congolese. Don't wait until the burr-
heads are forced into your schools. Do something about it
now!"

After the rally, more than a thousand of the crowd roamed
through the streets of downtown New Orleans, indiscrimi-
nately attacking blacks, and damaging cars, windows, and neon
signs. At least four blacks were hospitalized; police arrested
fifty of the rioters, and had to turn fire hoses on the crowd.
Bottles, bricks, and boards were hurled at passing cars driven
by blacks. A wad of burning newspaper was tossed into one
car; a large piece of ice was thrown through the window of a
bus by one of a group of white men, knocking a black woman
unconscious.

The public schools closed early for Thanksgiving; pressure
on the parents of the few remaining white pupils in Frantz and
McDonogh increased. The state legislature again declared the
school board dismissed, and attempted to withhold $1,262,000
from it, claiming that any checks it issued would be worthless.
Judge Wright issued another restraining order, which the legislators appealed to the U.S. Supreme Court as a matter of
"paramount importance." During the next few days, seven
hundred state officials—including Jimmie Davis, the governor
—were federally enjoined from interfering with desegregation.

When school resumed, only a few white parents and children had courage enough to come. These were jeered and spat

upon. Reporters and photographers were beaten. A Catholic priest accompanying a Methodist minister and his daughter to Frantz was called a bastard, a Communist, and a "nigger-lover." When the police arrived, the mob moved to the lawn of an adjacent house, chanting "Nigger-lover, nigger-lover, nigger-lover, Jew. We hate niggers, we hate you." Others waved Rebel flags and sang, "All I want for Christmas is a clean white school."

Although school board funds had been cut off, and its members threatened with arrest, they, the principals, and the teachers continued to report for work. The three federal judges struck down the concept of "interposition," and made it clear that an appeal by the state legislature would be useless. No public official, including the intrepid Governor Davis, seemed willing to go to jail for segregation, after all. In a last desperate attempt, the legislature passed a law written mostly by Perez permitting citizens of school districts to vote to abandon public schools faced with integration. The federal judges struck this down, and also ruled that state-aided private schools could not be a substitute for the public school system.

Perez did not confine himself to local problems. He wrote to President Eisenhower that "The widespread negro mob demonstrations in this country were planned many months ago. They plainly follow the same pattern as in Africa, and evidently are a part of the international Communist conspiracy and cold war to create turmoil, strife and national disunity. These negro mob actions . . . threaten the internal security of our country. . . . Would it not be in order for the President to request Congress to amend the presently pending Civil Rights bill in Congress to include a provision directed against continued Communist and pro-communist agitations in this country?" He wrote to Senator Eastland suggesting the proposal of a constitutional amendment that would permit separate but equal school facilities. Eastland wrote back, "I think the idea is fine and I expect to introduce this amendment in the very near future. I will also make a speech when I introduce it and would like to have your ideas on what I should say."

Perez addressed a "leadership meeting" at the Edgewater Gulf Hotel near Biloxi, Mississippi, attended by disgruntled Southern Democrats, during which he denounced the Supreme Court, a federal government supposedly infiltrated with Communists, Alger Hiss, the Carnegie Foundation, the Republican party, Latvia, Estonia, "the Mongol People's Republic," "the Ukrainian SSR and the USSR," the N.A.A.C.P., the American Jewish Congress, Lehman, Javits, Morse, "Emanuel Celler and other Fellow Travelers," Stalin, the Democratic party, the United Nations, the World Court, the Connally-Vandenberg Amendment, Fidel Castro, the Fair Employment Practices Commission, the American Communist Party, the U.S. Attorney General, the Congolese Constitution, the Russian Constitution, the Yugoslavian Constitution, "the Communist Constitution," the Communist Manifesto, Nelson Rockefeller, Henry Wallace, New York, Manhattan, Harlem, Walter Reuther, and Hubert Humphrey.

He concluded: "My friends, we have in our hands, if we would but use it, the power of a bloc vote far greater than that of any other . . . in this country. . . . Representatives of ten Southern states filed an emphatic dissent against the adoption of the pro-Communist civil rights plank in the Democratic platform. . . . Will the political leaders of these Southern states heed the demands of their people and back up that protest?"

Perez did not want to support either Richard Nixon or John Kennedy in the presidential election, and started a movement for the election of unpledged Democratic electors in Louisiana which he hoped would give the States' Righters bargaining power. In the Democratic state Central Committee his influence had diminished some, and in 1960 the committee was almost evenly divided between the conservatives, led by Perez, and the more liberal, loyal Democrats, led by a state senator from Baton Rouge named J. D. DeBlieux (pronounced like the letter W in Louisiana). Through DeBlieux's efforts a resolution had been passed by the Committee assigning the rooster symbol to the national Democratic ticket. "Everything seemed to be set," DeBlieux later recalled, "and then lo and behold, before the ballots could be printed, Perez goes and files suit in state court to deprive the national party of the rooster. He succeeded in getting the court to agree that the symbol belonged to the *Louisiana* Democrats."

The struggle for states' rights and all that included was, in Perez's eyes, far from over. Desegregation of sorts might have arrived in New Orleans, but he vowed that it would never happen in Plaquemines. First, though, he and three friends took ten days off for a bear hunt in British Columbia, which cost him two thousand dollars.

Perezbyteria

. . . ranking among the great legal minds of the Nation. . . . Fortunate in his heritage, fortunate in his character and fortunate in his happy and useful life, prompted continuously by the spirit of "noblesse oblige", Judge Leander Henry Perez takes upon his willing shoulders the burdens and responsibilities of numerous good works. . . . strong and resourceful, ready to meet every emergency with the conscientiousness that comes from a correct understanding of life's values and purpose and a true regard for the rights and privileges of others.

The Story of Louisiana,
*biographies of notable
citizens published in 1960*

Perez enjoyed pointing to Washington, D.C., as the prime example of a large American city "taken over" by black people. In the spring of 1961, with the assistance of F. Edward Hébert, Perez commissioned a private studio to make a film of black and white schoolchildren playing together. The Washington *Post* reported that the children were told by the filmmakers to fight and to throw rocks at each other. The film was shown that summer at a Citizens Council meeting in New Orleans presided over by Perez; also featured were mounted still photographs of black and white children mingling in the nation's capital.

Perez received bad news from Washington that fall, when F.B.I. agents entered Plaquemines and began to question residents about voter registration. Perez ran an ad in the Plaquemines *Gazette* saying that "two FBI agents are in Plaquemines Parish 'checking' on registration of voters for the 'Civil Rights' (?) Commission. Your registration is none of their business. Answer no questions. Tell them they are not welcome. Stand on your registration and right to vote."

The investigation caused attention outside the parish. Perez happily denounced the federal government to the newspapers, and was quoted—when asked if the *Gazette* ad was his idea— as saying, "It was my idea. Who the hell else has any ideas in Plaquemines?"

Perez immediately wrote angry letters to both New Orleans papers. He told the editor of the *States-Item*, "your paper quoted me as saying 'the federal government can go to hell.' That statement is typical 'poison pen' reporting. I did not make that statement. I said, 'Whoever gave the FBI the orders to harass our Plaquemines Parish voters can go to hell.' There is a whole lot of difference between that and the federal government. I know FBI Director Edgar Hoover did not give such an order."

To the editor of the *Times-Picayune*, Perez said, "I was misquoted as having said, 'Of course it was my idea * * * somebody's got to be planning down there. No one else gives a damn.' Your reporter tried to put words in my mouth which just don't fit. I did not and would not make such a statement. Our people are most cooperative and alert to their rights."

The Justice Department asked the federal court in New Orleans to instruct Plaquemines Parish officials to register Negro voters. The department pointed out that 6,714 of the 8,633 whites living in the parish were registered voters, while only 45 of the 2,897 Negroes were registered. At the hearing, Plaquemines registrar of voters Mary Ethel Fox was accused of applying different and more difficult qualification tests to Negroes. She was asked to demonstrate how she tested Negroes, and then to calculate her own exact age as required by the qualification test (Negroes were disqualified for miscalculating their age by as much as a single day). She miscalculated her own age by twenty-five days.

The courthouse clique apparently decided that a show of force was necessary in 1961. Perez had begun his fight for segregation believing in the efficacy of concerted legal resistance, but by now he was advocating "physical opposition." Early in the year he delivered the keynote address at an all-South Citizens Council meeting in Atlanta, where he called out the names of prominent members of the legislative, executive, and judicial branches of the federal government, referring to them alternately as "another pinko," "that Zionist," "a smart mulatto," and "that eighteen-time Commie front member." He said that the violent protests over desegregation in New Orleans marked "one of the most worthy demonstrations of a freedom-loving people. . . . How would you like it if your little girl came back home ravished from a forced racially integrated school?" To loud applause, whooping, and foot-stomping, Perez said that Southerners had no choice "but to rise up in physical opposition."

That year a group of armed deputies and members of the Plaquemines district attorney's office raided a black bar in the parish called the Chicken Shack. According to one witness, at least two raiders carried machine guns. The telephone was pulled out of the wall; bottles and glasses were shot off the bar and blasted from shelves behind it. More than one hundred patrons were forced to lie down on the floor, in the midst of broken glass and spilled beer and wine, where they were searched before being loaded into waiting school buses and taken to the jail at Pointe a la Hache, where they were charged with disturbing the peace.

The Associated Press heard about the incident, and through

it, the local branch of the N.A.A.C.P. up in New Orleans. Earl Amedee, who had previously assisted in the voter registration drive with Percy Griffin of the Plaquemines Parish Civic and Political Organization, and an assistant counsel for the N.A.A.C.P., A. M. Trudeau, Jr., decided to go down to Pointe a la Hache and defend those arrested. Amedee received a call from a black man who he later discovered was pro-Perez, telling him that a contact would meet him at the courthouse with a $150 retainer and the names of his clients.

When Amedee and Trudeau arrived at the Plaquemines courthouse, the contact was not there, and did not appear. Amedee didn't know that his prospective clients had already been persuaded to plead guilty; as he stood on the courthouse steps, waiting for court to open, a man behind him said, "What are you damn niggers doing down in this parish?"

Amedee and Trudeau turned and faced Perez, who was backed by a crowd of white men.

Amedee said, "You know me, Judge. I'm Earl Amedee."

"You're a liar," Perez said. "I don't know any goddamn niggers."

Amedee reminded Perez that he was an attorney, but Perez told him, "Don't give me any of that lawyer stuff. What are you doing down here?"

Amedee said that he was not required to say what case he was arguing, that information between a lawyer and his client was confidential.

"You're going to tell me," Perez said, "or I'll put you under the jail. You're a goddamn troublemaker sent down here by the N.A.A.C.P. to give whites trouble."

After Amedee admitted he had come down to defend those involved in the Chicken Shack incident, Perez told him that all the arrested Negroes had pleaded guilty. Amedee had no clients, and realized that he had been tricked.

"You mean the N.A.A.C.P. is interested in criminals and perverts?" Perez said. "Well, do you remember what happened to those Freedom Riders? That's nothing compared to what's going to happen to you."

Amedee remembers a group "of about fifteen crackers—and there wasn't a freejack [mulatto] among them. They all went into the general store. I knew how Klan members put a chaw of tobacco in their mouths and then drank a whole glass of bourbon, to kill their inhibitions. I knew they were going to kill us. . . . I started to pray, after telling Trudeau to get going, to drive five miles an hour less than the speed limit, but not to stop no matter what happened."

Fifteen miles above Pointe a la Hache was the north ferry crossing; Amedee wanted to take the ferry, but Trudeau wouldn't stop, and they continued north through St. Bernard Parish without being stopped. "By the time we got out, Trudeau was crying and saying how he was going to get some bad guys from the Seventh Ward in New Orleans and how they would kill every white person in Plaquemines. I just got out of the car in Orleans Parish and said, 'Lord, You know I've been fooling with that man [Perez] for ten years, and You know now that I'm not going back unless You tell me to.'"

He didn't.

The following March, Archbishop Rummel announced that parochial schools in the archdiocese would be desegregated; he was supported by the local priests. He sent out letters of "paternal admonition" to Perez and to other arch-segregationists, including Jackson Ricau, director of the South Louisiana Citizens Council, and Mrs. B. J. Gaillot, Jr., head of a racist group called Save Our Nation, threatening them with excommunication if they did not cease to encourage other Catholics to defy Rummel's ruling and to resist desegregation.

The newspapers printed a story about the letters, and Perez held his own press conference in New Orleans, at which he denied receiving any such letter from Rummel. And, he added, he would refuse to receive such a letter if anyone tried to deliver it. "The implication is condemnation to hell if a Catholic doesn't surrender his children to moral degradation. No sane person can understand that order." When asked by a reporter if he was suggesting that people stop supporting the churches, Perez asked him, "Would you contribute to those who would degrade your children? If you would, then you're not worthy of being a father." He said he had contributed "quite substantially" to two churches in Plaquemines whose priests' "morals and character are unquestionable." Referring to the threat of excommunication, he said, "I am a Catholic, and I intend to remain a Catholic."

Perez, Ricau, and Mrs. Gaillot (who with a crowd of supporters picketed the residence of Archbishop-Coadjutor John Patrick Cody carrying signs that read, "Will you answer to Christ your sins if we mix?" "The high priests made the same mistake. They repented. Will you?" and "Rebecca chose death rather than see her son integrate") were all excommunicated on April 16, 1962, for continuing their attempts to "provoke" opposition to desegregation of parochial schools. The priest sent to deliver the letter to Perez's home was forced to climb the fence because the gate was locked, and no one came to the door to receive the letter. Perez later claimed that because he had not personally received the papers, he wasn't legally excommunicated. He referred to the "purported ex-communications" as a "move to frighten or terrorize the parents of parochial students." He reaffirmed that he was "a life-long Catholic" and would continue to be one "regardless of communistic infiltration and the influence of the National Council of Christians and Jews upon our church leaders."

The following Sunday, Perez and Mama Perez attended mass at St. Joseph's Roman Catholic Church in Gretna, across the river from New Orleans, and both received communion. If the excommunication bothered Perez, he never indicated it, although Mama Perez was known to be upset by it, and fearful that Lélé would die outside the church. Perez even told an associate, "I had trouble with my archbishop. I said, 'If you think you can send me to hell, I'll ask you to go to hell!' Then a group of my friends organized our own church. We call it the *Perez*byterians."

He attended a meeting of the Parents and Friends of Catholic Children at a packed American Legion hall in New Orleans. Plainclothesmen circulated through the crowd, while uniformed policemen were stationed outside. Perez arrived in character: he was late, defiant, and buoyant, wearing a cowboy hat and smoking a cigar while handing out bumper stickers that read, "Better Ex-communication than Integration." The meeting opened with the saying of a Hail Mary. Before Perez spoke, Mrs. Gaillot stood and was applauded. She had already visited Rummel's residence, after announcing that she would appeal the excommunications to Rome; she had fallen to her knees before Rummel and told him, "Look up to heaven and admit you know it's God's law to segregate." She told the meeting, "We have crawled. We have pleaded. But this is our church, our religion, and we love it and will fight for it."

Perez told the crowd that excommunication "could send a Catholic to hell, but integration could send your children to a hell on earth." He encouraged them to "organize and fight," adding, "this is not a revolt against the Catholic Church. God forbid any such thought against Mother Church. . . . The Catholic Church is universal, and not what misguided temporal leaders say it is."

Rummel was, Perez said, telling a "bare-faced lie" by saying that segregation was sinful. Catholic bishops had been proved wrong in the past, he said, citing the examples of the burning of Joan of Arc and the torture of innocent persons during the Inquisition. "We are caught up in a spider web of international intrigue . . . with our church leaders taking their orders from Communists [who have] brainwashed our hierarchy."

Perez's difficulties with the church produced some interesting correspondence. A Jesuit in Pennsylvania wrote, on stationery emblazoned with the crest of the Knights of Malta, that as a Roman Catholic he saluted and congratulated Perez for his "courage" in fighting against desegregation. Archleader J. B. Stoner, writing beneath the letterhead of the Imperial Wizard of the Christian Knights of the Ku Klux Klan in Georgia, told Perez, "for many years I have worked with Catholics against the Jews and their communist and race-mixing conspiracies. . . . I am now writing an article for publication in The Klan Bulletin which will encourage Protestants and Catholics to work together against the Jew-communist race-mixers. In that article I will point out that the White Catholics of Louisiana have done more to preserve Segregation in the South than anybody else in Louisiana and that the White race is winning its struggle for survival in Louisiana as the result of Protestants and Catholics working together against the common enemy. For that article I would like to have a good picture of you. . . ."

Senator Eastland wrote to Perez quoting a letter from a friend in Rome suggesting that the Catholic Church had in fact been taken over by the Communist conspiracy. Eastland's friend had written: "The latest discouraging cloud on the horizon here is that the Vatican has been completely taken over by a Monsignor. He was a late-comer to the priesthood and was formerly an extreme Left reporter and broadcaster. He's now the major domo of the Vatican and makes all the policies for the Pope. Meanwhile, he screens all those seeking an audience and won't permit any right winger to see the old man. He has informed Catholic editors that the Church will have to coexist with Marxism just as they have coexisted for 500 years with the heresy of Protestantism! He also took a crack at Cardinal Mindszenty. Well, you can now account for the strange statements and actions coming from the Vatican. . . . What Catholics here are hoping is that the American Catholics will do something about it."

Perez did not neglect his other activities while dealing with the church fathers. One of his accomplishments was originating and backing a drive to stimulate the northward migration of blacks by providing them with free, one-way tickets to cities above the Mason-Dixon Line. The campaign was officially sponsored by the New Orleans Citizens Council and organized by Perez's satchel man, George Singelmann, who claimed to have sent hundreds of Negroes out of New Orleans. Only a handful of these departures could ever be confirmed. Singelmann and a secretary stuffed hundreds of application forms into envelopes in the Council office over the months, and sent them out to various black families; the response was less than expected, at a time when unemployment in the city was close to 7 per cent (30 per cent of this black), because black church leaders discouraged families from accepting the offer, calling it a "cruel joke." But Singelmann obviously thought he was providing a necessary service, and was proud of it. One night he even took his ten-year-old son to the Trailways bus station to see off an unemployed Negro seaman on his way to New York. Singelmann told reporters that his son "wanted to get his picture on TV, too."

Rummel was replaced as archbishop by his coadjutor, John Patrick Cody, who continued the effort to desegregate schools in the archdiocese. The target school in Plaquemines was Our Lady of Good Harbor, in Buras, where five black children were scheduled to start attending classes at the end of August. Earlier in the month, Perez spoke to another meeting of Catholic parents in New Orleans, and expressed the belief that Ricau and Mrs. Gaillot were "victims of circumstance. They were really aiming at me. . . . Well, I'm not any more ex-communicated than any of you here, because you've talked against [integration] just as much as I have. . . . If this ever does come to a test and I fail to stand up and do what I must do, my friends, I'm ready to lay down and die."

The announcement that black children would attend Our Lady of Good Harbor was almost more than Perez could believe. He told a group of Catholic parents in Buras, "Be there on opening day of school and watch the four or five little Negroes being paraded into your schools—the schools built with your contributions. Then take your children out of school. Then don't pay them a dime. . . . I urge you to cut off their water. . . . Your destiny lies in your own hands. May God give you the strength, the courage, the wisdom to do the right thing for yourselves and for your children."

The superintendent of the public schools, Sam Moncla, told the parents that they could bring their children to the public schools. "I am a Catholic," he said, "but when my church starts fighting me, I am going to fight back."

Perez was asked what guarantee he could provide that public schools would not be integrated. He drew loud applause when he answered, "I'm not here to give you any guarantees— you're here to join forces to fight for them. I can guarantee you only this. They won't have as easy a time integrating Plaquemines Parish as they have had in other places."

On August 29, five Negro children were escorted into Our Lady of Good Harbor. Thirty-eight white children also showed up for school, but soon left the building after a crowd of angry whites gathered outside. The Reverend Christopher Schneider, a gutsy Franciscan who intended to follow the instructions of his archbishop, threatened to close the school because of threats of violence to himself, the nuns, and some of the students' parents. He received no protection from sheriff's officers or the district attorney's office, though a few F.B.I. agents were present that first day, at the specific request of Attorney General Robert Kennedy (Perez called Kennedy "one of the Brothers K").

The Judge showed up at the school the second day and told the cheering crowd of whites that Archbishop Cody was a "hatchet man" sent by the Catholic Church to integrate schools, and that a three million dollar federal grant for an archdiocese housing development was the Kennedy administration's "pay-off" for parochial school desegregation. Perez added that Cody might "get his money, damn his hide, but he won't bluff Judge Perez and the people of Plaquemines Parish."

Harassment squads were assigned to the families of white children who continued to attend school; the squads called the homes of these families, attempting to convince them not to allow their children to return to school, and often threatening them. They also drove back and forth past their homes during most of the night. The sheriff's men went around to the homes of the blacks involved and requested that the children stay away from the school. One white man was so impressed by the threats against him that he took his family in a car at night and left the parish for good, carrying a revolver in his lap. The black children did not return to Our Lady of Good Harbor.

In New Orleans, 150 black pupils entered previously all-white parochial schools, and there were no incidents. The mayor and other city officials appeared on television, urging people to remain calm and promising that police would immediately arrest anyone trying to cause a disturbance. This reconciliation north of the parish line only hardened the resolve of Perez and his followers. The threats continued, and Father Schneider finally declared the school closed, after an increasingly hostile crowd gathered outside early in September. When Perez drove up and stepped out of his car, a white woman grabbed his hand and said, "God bless you, Mr. Perez," while onlookers applauded.

Perez addressed the crowd, urging them to resist desegregation efforts by either church or federal officials, and then he denounced what appeared to be a defeat in New Orleans for segregationist forces. "We built these schools. Not a dollar of federal or state money is in them. If they want to integrate our schools, they'll have to bring troops. . . . Did you see that bunch of sniveling cowards on television last night [in New Orleans]? They are a bunch of traitors and cowards who threatened to use the police force before anything happens But we won't sell you out here in Plaquemines." As he was leaving, Perez shouted at newsmen present, "If you're looking for yellow cowards, look someplace else!"

The worst was yet to come for Father Schneider and Our Lady of Good Harbor. He announced that the school would reopen on a thoroughly desegregated basis; days before that date, someone chained and padlocked the door. Father Schneider had to cut his way through with a hacksaw. He and the nuns were threatened with tarring and feathering. Then a nun received a telephone call from a white who said he intended to "blow up that school with you in it." Perez continued to admonish crowds around the school: "Cut off their water. Don't feed the fat bellies of the priests!"

Just before the school was to open, someone climbed onto the roof late at night and poured five gallons of gasoline down the stove vent. Around midnight the gasoline exploded without injuring anyone, but blowing out the windows and a wall, and charring the ceiling.

Archbishop Cody ordered the school closed; it never reopened.

Perez was later made the subject of a CBS television documentary called "The Priest and the Politician," which dealt mostly with the trouble at Our Lady of Good Harbor. Perez told the interviewer, "You're not going to make it seem that I would do anything improper. I do not decry activities of our people resisting in any way they can. . . . You're not going to have me say I'm against violence in self-defense. Violence in some cases is justifiable under law."

Perez described the CBS special contrasting him with Father Schneider as "corny" (he pronounced it "cawny"). In later years he assumed what was considered a more proper Southern accent, and often sounded remarkably like Edward G. Robinson with a Tidewater drawl. He also continued to go to church. He and Mama attended services at the Church of Our Lady of Perpetual Help in Belle Chasse, always arriving late, treating the occasion as a social one and, primarily, one for politicking. He sat at the rear of the church, in a special chair which bore the inscription "Usher."

In parish affairs, he moved in 1961 toward the total consolidation of his power by completely reorganizing the parish government. He abolished the Police Jury and replaced it with a smaller, more cohesive body known as the Commission Council; he called it a "charter form of local self-government" that provided the "only true home-rule in Louisiana." The preamble to the new charter began, "We, the people of Plaquemines Parish, Louisiana, grateful to Divine Providence for our many resources and opportunities, and to our patriotic founding fathers for our great heritage of liberty and freedom and of our constitutional form of government, which derive their [sic] just powers from the consent of the governed as the chief foundation stone of self-government, and is the heart and soul of the whole doctrine of States' Rights . . . ," and went on to stipulate that all Plaquemines residents would in the future be represented by five commissioners (instead of ten officials, as before). These were to be the commissioners of Public Affairs, Finance, Public Improvements, Public Safety, and Public Utilities; a Commission Council president and vice president would be elected from among the five commissioners.

It was obvious that the people of Plaquemines Parish had been deprived of half the representation they had had under the old ward system. The commission council form of government became popular in parishes split by the Mississippi River, but in Plaquemines's case the districts from which the commissioners were elected were greatly disproportionate in population and voting power. For instance, the commissioners of Public Affairs and Finance were forever to be elected from the east bank, representing only about ten per cent of the parish's population, and much of that black and non-voting. Whites living on the east bank—where Judge Perez, and later his second son, Chalin, maintained their official residences—were mostly landowners and almost universally pro-Perez.

The new charter also greatly minimized the political clout of the southern part of the parish—the traditional seat of the antis. Independent-minded citizens living below Pointe a la Hache found themselves lumped together with Perez supporters by the new district boundaries. The old Eighth Ward, which usually voted for the opposition, was completely abolished, "and we couldn't do anything about it," according to an anti living in Happy Jack. "We couldn't take a suit against the charter to the district court because the Perezes would file bills of exception on each of the fifteen sections in the charter, and then slap on an intervenor to delay things for years. The Court of Appeals is controlled, and it's difficult and expensive even to get into the state supreme court."

The Perez succession was assured. Before his excommunication, the Judge announced that he was resigning as district attorney of Plaquemines, after serving in that position for thirty-six years, and that he would be succeeded by his oldest son, Leander, Jr., who was then assistant district attorney. The Democratic executive committee immediately nominated Leander Perez, Jr.—commonly known as Lea—for the office of district attorney, and he ran unopposed in the next election. The Judge stipulated that he was remaining on the staff as assistant district attorney, "with all the powers of the District Attorney under the Constitution."

Perez was elected to the new Commission Council and became its first president by unanimous vote. Chalin was to take over those duties when the Judge decided it was time; until then he worked in Perez's law firm, and often advised members of the courthouse clique in his father's absence. The home built for Chalin on the east bank formally established his residence there, though in fact he lived in uptown New Orleans, as had his father, and as did Leander, Jr. The Judge eventually changed his official residence in Plaquemines to the west bank, when Promised Land was converted into a private white "academy" for the children of parents who would not allow them to attend desegregated schools. Perez had always wanted to move back to the west bank, where he was born; he and Mama Perez occupied the clapboard house on the sprawling Idlewild ranch, and gave Lea, Jr., an adjoining plot of land to the north. But when Lea began to build an imposing brick residence on his land, the Judge quickly commissioned an even more impressive brick plantation home with heavy columns, a fountain and patio, and eventually a family mausoleum in the back, shaded by massive oaks hung with Spanish moss. His home was finished before Lea's, which seemed to give the Judge considerable satisfaction, and he furnished it with exquisite antiques, many of them from exclusive shops along Royal Street in New Orleans, including two massive four-poster beds.

When the Judge stepped down as district attorney, a testimonial dinner was held at the Roosevelt Hotel in New Orleans. Nearly a thousand people came to pay tribute. Governor Davis presented him with a card that entitled him to exceed the speed limit on trips up to Baton Rouge; various speakers lavished praise upon him, likening him to Washington, Jefferson, Lincoln, Wilson, and the Roosevelts (in importance, not policy). F. Edward Hébert called Perez "the noblest Roman of them all," and "the Father of Plaquemines Parish."

"History is not written by indecisive Milquetoast figures," Hébert intoned, "but by controversial men who had something to say. [Perez] is like Tennyson's brook: 'Men may come and go, but I go on forever.' "

Perez was seventy, but he didn't look it. His capacity for outrage was as great as ever; with his rampant white pompadour, gold-rimmed spectacles, extraordinarily constant gaze, and stocky, well-preserved physique, Perez was still an impressive figure. (The woman editor of the Plaquemines Gazette later admitted, "It's a shame that a man of his age had so much sex appeal.") Perez rose and told the gathering that he was stepping down as district attorney so that he could devote more time to segregationist activities. He warned his friends against the pursuit of factional politics and advised them "to close ranks against the common enemy and Fellow Travellers who would force unmoral racial integration upon our children to destroy their education, their personal safety and well-being, and who would destroy our white civilization, so that in the end our nation may be easy prey to the Communist vultures. United we stand. Divided we fall!"

Chapter Six

The Lost Cause

Southern political personalities, like sweet corn, travel badly. They lose flavor with every hundred yards away from the patch.

A. J. Liebling,
The Earl of Louisiana

Alarms and Excursions

In the summer of 1963, Perez took on the federal government —or at least its representative in Plaquemines, which was the Naval Air Station at Belle Chasse, just a few miles from Idlewild ranch. The cause of the dispute was the release of a study, largely attributed to Washington attorney Gerhard A. Gesell, of racial discrimination in the United States armed forces, which suggested that military officers "showing initiative and achievement" in ending discrimination in the various services should receive special consideration for promotion. Perez loudly denounced the Gesell Report, after Secretary of Defense Robert McNamara issued on July 26 a directive implementing its recommendations. The directive stated: "Every military commander has the responsibility to oppose discriminatory practices affecting his men and their dependents and to foster equal opportunity for them, not only in areas under his immediate control, but also in near-by communities where they may live or gather in off-duty hours." The directive added that commanders might declare off-limits any areas where "relentless discrimination persists."

Perez took the offensive. He announced that parish schools would bar the children of base personnel—about 100 children. The base was actually nothing more than a reserve training facility housing 650 military personnel and about 500 civilian employees. The base had never sought to enroll black children in Plaquemines's schools, and Perez's announcement caused apprehension on the base, consternation among the military in general, and great interest among average citizens and the press. Perez later modified his statement about the base's children, saying that they would be admitted for that year but perhaps not for the following one; after the August meeting of the Commission Council, however, he did declare Plaquemines Parish generally off-limits to other base personnel.

Newspaper and television reporters gathered inside the courthouse at Pointe a la Hache and listened while Perez denounced, and demanded a congressional investigation of, the Gesell Report, which, he said, instructed military commanders "to invite a more or less equal number of Negro girls for social on-base functions, and fewer girls—or ladies—who believe in segregation." He then announced that all bars and lounges, as well as other business establishments, in Plaquemines were off-limits to uniformed base personnel; George Singelmann proudly termed this "the public accommodations law in reverse."

The government had threatened economic reprisal against communities where resolute discrimination existed. Perez responded: "We say the hell with you, the United States government! . . . The Pentagon is discouraging Negro servicemen from seeking the company of their own race and encouraging them to push themselves on white girls. And you know what would happen if Negroes pursued white girls in Plaquemines."

Rear Admiral Charles Lyman, in charge of the base but stationed in New Orleans, issued a statement that was extraordinarily imaginative by military standards. "In Navy parlance," he said, "we were sitting peaceably on our sea bags, gazing out the porthole, when we were whacked over the head by this reported threat. . . . I stand ready to go to Central Quarters [battle stations], while hoping that sensible people both in Plaquemines Parish and elsewhere will stand up on their hind legs and prevent any such foolishness."

Neither Perez nor the Pentagon was amused by Admiral Lyman's statement, and he was silent thereafter. It was under-

135

stood that any decision declaring Plaquemines off-limits to military personnel would come from Washington. (No such decision was ever made.) Perez received many letters and telegrams from admirers throughout Louisiana and the South ("Thank you for your application of the Gisselle [sic] Report in reverse." "Congratulations from Florida, would be privileged to meet you." "This is the best thing you have done yet. May I help?" "Keep up the good work. We are behind you 100 per cent in Alabama." "Many of us glory in you [sic] spunk. I have thought of doing the same thing as far as my business is concerned, and will if pressure is applied in our area." "Congratulations on your masterful display of 'one-upsmanship' in your recent 'off-limits' statement! It looks like you caught the other side off balance!").

Perez continued to blast both McNamara's directive and the Gesell Report. He referred to it variously as "the Negro Gesell Report," "the Gesell-Yarmolinsky Conspiracy," and "the Yarmolinsky-McNamara Report." The name of Adam Yarmolinsky, McNamara's assistant, fascinated Perez, and he pronounced it with elaborate hissing sounds that his underlings at the courthouse must have assumed was the essence of malevolent Russian pronunciation. Perez's directive never really affected the personnel at the Belle Chasse base, since they preferred to drink up in New Orleans; if they wanted to drink in Plaquemines, they simply went into bars in civilian clothes.

The ordinance went into effect in early September. WWL television in New Orleans said in an editorial, "Any bar owner in the parish selling or even giving a Coke to a man in uniform . . . could be fined twenty-five dollars and put in jail for thirty days. You're right—it is just as funny as it sounds. But it was not intended to be funny. This is the answer of the parish Council—or more specifically, the answer of Leander Perez—to the Gesell Report. . . . If there is any humor to be found in this, we suppose it is the sight of Mr. Perez being so righteously outraged at the idea of someone using such dictatorial tactics."

Perez was determined to prevent a liberal national Democratic party from getting Louisiana's electoral votes in the presidential election of 1964. Early in the year he backed John McKeithen (whose campaign slogan was, "Won't ya please hep me?") in the second state gubernatorial primary against the more liberal "Chep" Morrison, former mayor of New Orleans and an old Perez foe. Perez sent out a letter to Plaquemines voters informing them that the primary would "decide the fate of the white man's position in State government. Chep Morrison . . . received the total negro bloc vote of over 130,000 in the First Primary, thus definitely establishing Morrison as the NAACP-CORE-MARTIN LUTHER KING CANDIDATE. . . . McKeithen has come out positively against federal government interference with our State affairs. McKeithen is in favor of giving the people the right to vote in the Democratic Party Primary election for Presidential Electors, with the freedom of choice between one slate of electors for the anti-South Presidential Nominee of the National Democratic Convention, and one slate of electors for an outstanding independent candidate for president. . . . Regardless of paid endorsements, THE PEOPLE CANNOT BE BOUGHT. The challenge which now faces every citizen of Louisiana is unmistakable. It is—Shall we have a Communist-controlled NAACP-CORE-MARTIN LUTHER KING dominated state government?"

Although it was no longer such a common practice among reactionary Southern politicians to denounce their enemies as Communists, Perez continued unabated. He had gone so far as to appeal to the Democratic state Central Committee to ask Louisiana's congressional delegation to vote against Kennedy's omnibus farm bill, on the grounds that the bill's provisions for agrarian reform were similar to methods used in China and Cuba. Senator Russell Long, Perez's enemy since the Dixiecrat days, called Perez's argument "a lot of folderol, a lot of fraudulent issues. People are tired of being called Communists just because they don't agree with you. You call President Eisenhower, President Kennedy a Communist, Archbishop Rummel, Pope John a Communist. It's getting so it will be respectable to be called a Communist."

McKeithen was elected, giving Perez a valuable friend in

the state, particularly since, under a new law, McKeithen would be the first governor to be able to succeed himself in office. Whether or not McKeithen's election decided the fate of the white man's position in state government, as Perez contended, it did nothing to minimize civil rights activity in Louisiana. Perez received a letter from Ronnie Moore of the Congress of Racial Equality, who was up in the town of Plaquemine, north of Baton Rouge, taking part in voter registration efforts there. (One explanation for the fact that CORE workers went to the town of Plaquemine first, instead of down into Plaquemines Parish as they were supposedly instructed to do, is that they could save face by pretending to have misunderstood those instructions. Members of CORE who were in the town of Plaquemine in 1964 deny this.) Moore wrote to Perez that "public accommodations can no longer be maintained on a racially segregated basis," and promised "to commence non-violent direct action to attain the objectives of a community open to all of its citizens . . . unless there is voluntary compliance with provisions of the Civil Rights bill."

Perez's reaction was not as emotional as might be imagined. He wrote back to Moore, saying, "We do not recognize CORE as having any right to make demands of any kind upon us. I know that CORE is heavily infiltrated with Communists, among its directors particularly. We will not condone any Communist-directed activities in Plaquemines Parish. . . . If CORE should come into Plaquemines Parish under the guise of racial non-violent protest, we can only consider this CORE's intention to stir up violence . . . and you and CORE would meet with a reception befitting its communistic role to stir up racial strife, turmoil and violence and disunity."

Perez told a crowd in Plaquemines, at the dedication of a local pumping station, not to worry about CORE's threat. He said that if outside demonstrators should come, "we are prepared to handle them in a different way. We have some surprises in store for them." He urged his fellow citizens "to be courageous and not to surrender to the Communist regimentation which makes up the Civil Rights bill, but to stand together and be worthy to be called Americans." Perez had not yet announced how he would handle demonstrators; his approach would prove to be definitely "different."

Perez spent a great deal of time speeding between Plaquemines Parish and Baton Rouge. He had found the "outstanding independent candidate for president" he had mentioned in the letter to his constituents—Alabama's George Wallace—and he planned to see Wallace, not President Johnson, on Louisiana's Democratic ballot. Perez wrote to a friend saying that "Governor Wallace is doing a great job awakening the conscience of the American people to the need for saving constitutional government in this country as against the progressive socialist-communist aggression." That meant, in plain language, that Wallace was the most acceptable candidate to the old Dixie-crats and current States' Righters.

In April, Perez went to Baton Rouge with Singelmann to lead the fight within the state central committee against the loyalist Democratic faction. More than two hundred demonstrators, many of them Citizens Council members from northern Louisiana, lined the sides of the House chamber in the Capitol, and cheered Perez on. They carried placards reading, "Vote Yes For Wallace," "Save Segregation—Vote States' Rights—Unpledged Electors," and "Save Us from L.B.J. (Light Bulb Johnson)—Free Electors for '64." Cards were also distributed in support of Perez's efforts, urging, "You don't have to vote for free electors! You have two other choices: You can vote for: 1. Military dictatorship under the Democrats. 2. Military dictatorship under the Republicans. Stay free with free electors!"

A former state senator was elected chairman of the committee with the support of Perez and of prominent McKeithen backers. He ruled repeatedly in favor of Perez during the hour-and-a-half battle over who was to get the rooster. The loyalists then attempted to repeal a previously passed Perez resolution calling for a preferential primary in July in which two ten-man slates of presidential electors named by the central committee would run. The winning slate would then be placed on the

November general election ballot under the rooster symbol, which some claimed was still worth 100,000 votes. Perez contended that this provision would give the Democrats in Louisiana a choice between the national party ticket and Governor Wallace. The plan, and its variations in Alabama and Mississippi, had no hope of achieving real success except in a very close national election. Its objective was to deny either party candidate the required majority of electoral votes and throw the election into the House of Representatives, where Southerners believed they could obtain concessions on the racial issue.

Johnson was not assured a place on the Louisiana ballot, even if he became the Democratic nominee. The loyalists attempting to repeal Perez's old resolution met with shouted opposition, both from the demonstrators and from the Judge himself, who with considerable oratory proposed his own substitute motion for the motion to repeal the free elector rule. This failed to carry, but Perez then pushed through a motion to adjourn, and the free elector rule remained. He was obviously pleased with the outcome of the meeting. When asked by a reporter if the committee's action had dashed hopes that Louisiana would support Johnson in November, Perez thundered, "We want Lyndon B. Johnson to come before the million or more people of Louisiana and say, 'I want you to vote for me despite what I'm doing to you.' The people of Louisiana would give him a kick in the pants!"

McKeithen's apparent support of the Perez faction was not so much in the interest of states' rights as it was an effort to obtain agreement in the offshore oil dispute from President Johnson—a situation that was never without interest for Perez either. Approximately $641 million from Gulf oil lands was being held in escrow, and a large part of that would go to the state after the boundary was finally settled. A few days before, McKeithen had conferred with Johnson on this very problem. Oil and states' rights were still very much companion issues.

To Johnson's threat of cutting off federal aid to school districts failing to desegregate, Perez responded by calling on all

Southerners to challenge Johnson before the November election. In a television interview filmed at the courthouse at Pointe a la Hache, Perez said, "Let's see where the cowards are. It will either be LBJ, the Texas Renegade, or the state and local government officials." He claimed that Robert Kennedy, with President Johnson's support, encouraged rioting by blacks. "Because of the white backlash, the Texas Renegade says that he wants to enforce laws against racial riots. So they have arranged a 'moratorium' on racial demonstrations until *after* the election. Then all hell will break loose. It will be open warfare of the Communist-dominated Negro organizations against certain cities in the South. . . . Let's see how much federal coercion will be used. Let's make them use it. Let's find out just how near we really are to the Communist Manifesto type of government."

Asked his opinion of Barry Goldwater, Perez said, "If I read Goldwater right, he is a product of the wide open spaces. He has strength. He is a good American, dedicated to Constitutional government. He is also a politician rubbing elbows with northern liberals. . . . He may be versatile enough to use some of their own language. Let's put it simply—when you talk with an s.o.b., you talk s.o.b. language. . . . If you saw the picture of Eisenhower in the morning paper, with his meaningless smile, and Goldwater's [photograph], you will have noticed that Goldwater was gritting his teeth. He showed his strength of character. I don't believe that Goldwater can be a captive in his own mansion, as Eisenhower was."

The interview was covered by the New Orleans newspapers, as well as by the Plaquemines *Gazette*, which never failed to print any public statement by Perez. The *Gazette* reported that Perez had accused his old enemy, Hale Boggs, of advocating one-world government, and went on to explain to its readers that "in a one-world government, which would be controlled by a world parliament, all countries would have representatives in that government in accordance with their populations. Since the United States has just about a 190 million population, its representatives would be dominated by the greater number of representatives of Russia and its Satellites with its half-billion population, India with its almost half-billion population, China with its six hundred million, Africa with its millions, and other large populated countries. This would mean that the United States . . . would be the minority country."

Perez said in the interview that the choice of the Democratic Vice Presidential candidate would be dictated by David Dubinsky, who, according to the *Gazette*, "contrals 400,000 Communist votes in the Communist Party," and by " 'Yours-for-a-Soviet-America' Walter Reuther." Perez was asked, "What can you do? Throw in the towel?" The Judge just grinned and shook his head. "That's not like Perez," he said.

Perez later told an audience of Citizens Council members in St. Bernard not to accept federal aid to schools. "Our people haven't really matured," he said. "They haven't grown up. They haven't learned the first law of nature—self-preservation. . . . The white people are going to have to close ranks and learn a lesson from CORE and NAACP and Martin Luther King, to stick together to save our civilization. . . . The people have to save themselves. The Legislature has authorized school boards to submit a one-cent sales tax to meet the need for funds taken away. The question is for people to decide if they will sell their children down the river."

Perez's "different way" of dealing with civil rights demonstrators was finally unveiled in the early summer of 1964. On a hot, gusty afternoon, a dozen men—most of them reporters and photographers—boarded a shrimp trawler thirty miles up from the mouth of the Mississippi and set out for the east bank. Among them was Perez, cigar and cigar holder clamped in his teeth, wearing a suit and tie and carrying his lunch in a paper bag. He bantered with the newsmen in a manner that was both courtly and aggressive; whatever the newsmen's opinion of Perez, they all seemed to be enjoying themselves by the time they reached the edge of low, stone battlements topped with barbed wire. This was old Fort St. Philip, built by the Spanish in 1746 on a knob of firm ground surrounded by water, swamp, and marshland. It resembled an elaborate cattle pen, accessible only by water: a nine-foot fence of hog wire topped by three electrified strands contained an open courtyard partially shaded by ash and hackberry trees. The guard shack, a Quonset-hut type of structure resting on top of a cannon emplacement, was empty. Beneath each emplacement, dank powder magazines with low ceilings had been converted into cells; some had water standing in the floors, and all harbored swarms of large swamp mosquitoes. The reporters, though daubed with insect repellent, slapped the backs of their necks and hands as the Judge led them through his new prison, which had been leased by the parish the year before.

Perez called the ersatz concentration camp "preventative medicine," and so far it had kept out CORE workers, at least. Asked if he thought conditions in the prison were inhumane, he said, "All prisons are made of concrete and steel, and this one won't even have any doors," which it wouldn't need because escape was almost impossible. He added that the electric fences could be regulated "to anything the doctor orders."

The group stopped in the middle of the courtyard, and Perez joined reporters in picking fruit from a spreading mulberry tree. "If every area would prepare like we have," he told them, "you'd see a lot less racial trouble. . . . I don't think we'll ever use this place. The northern Negro leaders expect the local people to handle it [the demonstrations], and we have a peaceful group of Negroes around here. Oh, there are some who would like to kick up their heels, but we know who they are, and they won't move. You know, this place isn't for Negroes only—it's for anarchists, those who come here to overthrow the legally constituted government. If whites choose to agitate with Negroes, they'll come here too. There won't be any discrimination."

Perez then went up to the guard shack to eat his lunch in the shade.

The election of Lyndon Johnson in November came as no surprise to Perez. He told a group of students in Port Sulphur that "the grown-ups of the nation showed their lack of understanding of government when they voted." He attacked politics as "the sinful game of fooling the people." Government, however, was "a business. . . . We must always support government. When government supports its people, the people become vassals of the state." He then admitted that he hated "politics—the curse of the country," and likened politics to an old brand of flypaper: "This paper was coated with a substance which attracted flies. They came and they ate and they got caught."

Perez received a unique opportunity to loudly protest "federal encroachment" and to defend Plaquemines's "way of life" early the next year. The Senate Judiciary Committee conducted hearings on the 1965 voting rights bill, and Governor McKeithen agreed to let Perez represent him and Louisiana at the hearings. McKeithen gave as his excuse for not appearing the fact that he had to be in Chicago on another industry-promoting trip for the state. So the Judge was chosen to present McKeithen's position that individual states should be allowed to set voting qualifications; the new governor would regret the choice.

Perez traveled to Washington, accompanied by Luke Petrovich, Plaquemines's Commissioner of Public Safety; on Tuesday, March 30, Perez was called upon by Senator James O. Eastland, his old buddy from Mississippi and chairman of the Senate Judiciary Committee. Perez began by attacking the constitutionality of the Voting Rights Act of 1965, and by claiming that the bill's provision to take away the rights of certain states to fix their own voter qualifications was aimed specifically at the Deep South, because often less than 50 per cent of the registered voters in those states had voted in the last election. (The Voting Rights Act authorized federal intervention in those states with less than 50 per cent voting.) Asked by Eastland why Louisiana's vote in the November election had been so low, Perez answered that it was because Louisiana voters opposed the Democratic platform, and were "allergic to voting Republican. . . . The big majority of our people are good, conservative, patriotic, constitutional Americans. We do not subscribe to the principles of the Americans for Democratic Action, the Marxist-Socialist front. That is why our people refrained from going to the polls in large numbers. I might cite here our reaction. On a trip out to South Dakota, I stopped at the railroad station in Chicago and I met a florid-faced little Irish lawyer-politician, who tackled me and said, 'How are things going in Louisiana?' during the campaign. I said, 'About 60–40 Goldwater.' 'Why,' he said, 'Man, you are crazy. You don't know what you are talking about.' I said, 'Mister, you are talking to a man who knows what he is talking about when he is talking about Louisiana. Our vote is nearly 60–40.' He said, 'You are going on a pheasant hunt. Aren't you doing well? Aren't you satisfied that the country is prosperous?' I said, 'Mister, in Louisiana most of us do not play belly politics, we use reasoning.' "

Perez said Plaquemines Parish had been "discriminated" against when federal suit was brought against Mary Ethel Fox, the registrar of voters, and he had the federal district court's decision placed in the record. Senator Eastland asked Perez if he didn't think allegations of intimidation of black people wanting to vote in the South were "largely a myth," and Perez said, "I said it was nefarious, willful, malicious, lying propaganda." He called the voting rights bill "worse than the Thaddeus Stevens legislation during Reconstruction . . . the most nefarious. It is inconceivable that Americans would do that to Americans." He attacked some specific provisions of the bill, read from Charles Collins's *Whither Solid South* about the horrors of Reconstruction (". . . an attempt to destroy white civilization in the South by crude and brutal methods . . . the carpetbagger stalked the stricken South like a jackal to filch for himself something from the wreckage"), and announced that he was including in the record a copy of the constitution of the Union of Soviet Socialist Republics, because in Russia eighteen-year-olds were also allowed to vote, so "let's imitate Russia." He rather incoherently lamented the fact that the new voting rights bill had no "moral qualifications. I do not know why, except from what we hear about Washington, with all the queers and everything in government positions, thousands and thousands of them. . . . The perverts, the unmoral people, the aliens—persons. After all, they are persons. And we should be dedicated to upholding the dignity of man. Human rights."

Perez then tossed down the Russian constitution with a flourish. Such testimony was bound to attract attention in the usually sedate atmosphere of a committee hearing; Perez was just warming up. He said the bill was part of a "Black Belt Communist conspiracy . . . laid out by Stalin," and to prove it he included in the record a document put out by the Patrick Henry Group of Virginia called *Is the NAACP Subversive?*—a lengthy evaluation of various N.A.A.C.P. members which attempted to link them with the Communist party. He also included various other right-wing publications, including the *Baptist Bible Tribune* and *Common Sense.*

The committee recessed for lunch. The afternoon session was to be more acrimonious than the morning one: Perez introduced more "evidence" that civil rights workers, including Martin Luther King, were associated with Communists; part of his evidence was a pamphlet put out by the Workers Library Publishers entitled *American Negro Problems.* Senator Eastland assumed the role of foil to Perez, so that the latter could make any type of statement he chose. At one point Perez said of the bill, "Do you not see the Communist plan back of this thing? I do not hesitate to call it that, because that is what it is. I challenge anyone to debate it with me. . . . The Communist fronts . . . are sponsoring these mass actions and demonstrations that are creating all of this hysteria in the country."

Everett Dirksen of Illinois spoke up. "Now, Mr. Perez, that is about as stupid a statement as has ever been uttered in this hearing, and it is a reflection upon members of the Senate."

"Sir," Perez said, "I would say that this is a reflection upon the members of Congress if they give this type of legislation serious consideration."

"Well, that is not what you said. Now let us have the reporter read back your remark."

Perez's statement was read back, and Dirksen suggested that he take the statement about the Communist plan out of the record. Perez said that he had "no objection," then asked that the remark be stricken; "But I still say that the exhibits that I have filed can be used to make the point."

Senator Hugh Scott of Pennsylvania told the committee, "I did not think anybody could out-do the Birch Society, but I am afraid Mr. Perez does it."

Dirksen later pointed out that in Plaquemines Parish only 3.3 per cent of the black population was registered to vote, and told Perez, "there is something radically wrong down there."

"Do you want me to tell you further what is radically wrong?" Perez said. "We worked to get our people registered, and I will admit that we do not go out and beat the bushes to register the Negroes. You know why? In the adjoining parish of St. Bernard in my judicial district there is about 800 Negroes registered in every election. You have got to pay them off. You have got to bribe them. You have got to pay the preachers. . . ."

By this time Dirksen and some other senators were laughing. Dirksen asked Perez who bribed the preachers, and Perez told him, "That is not a funny question, sir," and said it was the candidates who had to do the bribing. He then lamented the large number of "illegitimate children" among Negroes, and described them as "a low type of citizenship. They do not have the ambition, they do not have the urge, they do not know enough about government, they do not care. They are being well treated. . . ."

When Perez later reasserted that his parish should be able to set its own voter qualifications, Dirksen asked, "Is Plaquemines Parish in orbit somewhere?"

Perez said, "No, sir. That is not funny either. Plaquemines Parish is not in orbit, sir, but Plaquemines Parish has certain rights under the Constitution."

Senator Philip Hart of Michigan asked Perez if he really believed that members of Congress were acting as agents of foreign powers.

"Of course not," Perez said. "None of my remarks, I hope, will be taken in a personal way. I am only analyzing the bill. . . . I have devoted a good deal of time to this question of Communist infiltration. I remember when the Supreme Court handed down that decision in March 1954. I could smell it. . . . I came up here and with certain other help we dug into the question of the Communist background of the authorities cited by the court, especially Gunnar Myrdal's book. . . . I have done a great deal of work on that and I am not going to be fooled. I know the result of this thing. I know how it will fit in with the Black Belt conspiracy, and I do not question the motives of anyone. I am only looking to the painful results of this type of legislation."

Hart said, "It just strikes me as absolutely nuts to suggest that . . ."

"Absolutely what?" Perez asked.

"Nuts."

"N-u-t-s?"

"Nuts to suggest," Hart continued, "that those engaged in seeking to broaden the exercise of the franchise in a free society are doing something that should be questioned."

Hart asked Perez if he condoned night-riding, and Perez said that he did not, but that other people committed crimes in the South, and cited cases of blacks attacking whites. He pointed out that crime was worse in the North than in the South, and told a story about walking with Mama Perez "within a block of the nation's Capitol" and being warned by two policemen that "it was not safe for a man and his wife to walk peacefully along the boulevard." Crime, Perez said, was part of "the orders of the Comintern to stir up strife and national disunity," as was the proposed voting rights bill.

"What do you expect will happen in the South when the federal government tries to impose Negro rule on the South in the second Reconstruction? Why was the Klan born during Reconstruction times? To defend white women. . . . It is our women that we have to protect, and we are going to protect them, and if the people have to go underground, that is where they are going."

Perez ended his testimony by giving an example to illustrate his contention that human beings were naturally segregated according to color and even hue: "I remember when I was a young fellow and my father hired a young mulatto boy as his chauffeur. And he took his cousin who was rather dark to a mulatto dance down [in Plaquemines] and they beat the stew out of him and ran him out of the dancehall because he was black. And that is the way it goes. No act of Congress is going to change that."

Senator Eastland thanked Perez, and said, "You have made a very fine statement and raised some questions that this committee has got to give consideration to."

Perez and his companion Petrovich went back to Louisiana, where Perez was assailed by reporters asking why he had withdrawn his charge of Communist influence backing the voting rights bill. Perez was outraged. "I didn't take back a damn thing. They didn't like to have the smell of Communism rubbed into the nostrils, but I rubbed it in." He claimed he said to Dirksen regarding the statement about Communist influence, "If you feel offended, if you want to take it out, take it out. But Dirksen didn't order it stricken. It rested there. Is that backtracking?"

Governor McKeithen was understandably upset by Perez's flamboyant testimony. Contacted by reporters in Chicago, Mc-Keithen said that Perez had been authorized only "to state our position that the matter [voting requirements] should be left to the states, and that literacy tests are essential, but no person should be disallowed to vote because of his color. Judge Perez hasn't carte blanche to make statements for me impugning the motives of those in favor of federal legislation."

Perez retorted, "I didn't ask the Governor what to say. It's natural he would not be as forthright and as comprehensive as I."

Perez was clearly alarmed that the people of Louisiana

might think he had been bested and ridiculed by members of the Judiciary Committee. When a reporter asked him about his derogatory statements about blacks, Perez snapped, "Do you know what the Negro is? An animal right out of the jungle. Passion, welfare, easy life—that's the Negro. And if you don't know that, you're naive."

He bought time on statewide television—paid for by the Plaquemines Parish Commission Council—to "explain" the Voting Rights Act of 1965 as his "public duty," and to give his version of what had transpired in Washington. Perez called the bill "nefarious" and "a fraud." He then said of Senator Hart, who had called Perez's remark "nuts": "The man showed fear. He was noticeably shaky. You could feel the hysteria which seemed to grip him. And no wonder. He was a Senator from Walter Reuther's state." Of other senators on the committee, Perez said, "You could tell what they feared above all was the threat of a Martin Luther King or CORE demonstration at their Senate office door, or in their home town, which might liquidate them politically."

He then claimed—falsely—that "I really don't know if anything I said was stricken from the record. I did not withdraw or back down from anything I said. . . . Let's not be fooled by the way the news media carried this Senator Dirksen matter to obscure the whole outrageous nature of this Martin Luther King bill against our six Southern states and the troubles and hardships which are in store for our people as a result of this kind of outrageous, unconstitutional law."

Perez never got over his encounter with Dirksen. His critics said that Perez's statement before the committee was dramatic proof of his growing political obsolescence. In state affairs, he was still powerful within the Democratic Central Committee, but the loyalist faction led by DeBlieux was gaining the upper hand. Perez's break with the national Democrats was irreparable, and now he rejected the Republicans. Later that year in a letter to D. Bruce Evans, director of the United Republicans of America, Perez said, "You might recall that when I appeared before the Senate Judiciary Committee against the so-called

'Voting Rights Act of 1965', I re-emphasized that the enactment
of such a law would give impetus to the communist program,
[and] Republican Senator Dirksen said that such a statement
was 'stupid.' Senator Dirksen got quite a lot of advertisement
out of that comment of his. . . . I am sure it will be conceded
that I helped materially in the large majority which Louisiana
gave to Barry Goldwater in the past Presidential election, but
how can I justify myself in supporting the next Republican
Party presidential candidate while its recognized leaders make
common cause with the communist conspiracy and the Democratic Party leaders . . . ?"

Enemies at the Ranch

*"What are you going to do now, Leander?
The Feds have got the atom bomb."*

Earl Long

The early 1960's were violent times in Plaquemines Parish. The
fire-bombing of Our Lady of Good Harbor in Buras was the
one big defeat of the attempt by the Catholic Church to desegregate schools within the archdiocese. Elsewhere, progress
was made in desegregating the parochial schools, but not without opposition in Plaquemines. When Rev. Frank Ecimovich of
Our Lady of Perpetual Help in Belle Chasse began to give
religious instruction to mixed groups of black and white children, he was abused by parents in the area. Four of them went
to the rectory to attempt to discourage the mixed classes, and
when they failed, one of the men slugged Ecimovich, leaving
him with a highly visible black eye.

Burnings of Negro property were fairly common. Percy
Griffin, black leader on the east bank and founder of the old
Civic and Political Organization, woke up one night to find his
house in Phoenix surrounded by flames. The fire was caused by
what he described as "walking oil," a mixture of gunpowder

and crude oil, which was trailed completely around his house and out to the road, where it was ignited. A carload of white men sped away; Griffin managed to put out the blaze before the house burned.

Across the river in Boothville, the recognized black leader, Sam Taylor, a well-built mulatto preacher with light blue eyes, lost his car when arsonists doused it with gasoline, and set it afire. A year later, Taylor was standing at his bedroom window one night when a wall of flame leaped up beside the house. In the blaze he saw a white man holding a five-gallon gasoline can fall backwards from the force of the flames; the gasoline he had been spreading around the house had been accidentally ignited by the pilot flame on the outdoor hot water heater. Taylor watched as the arsonist, charred and panicked, ran into a thorn tree trying to escape, and finally dove into the canal behind Taylor's property and swam off into the darkness. Taylor put out the fire before his house was destroyed; the sheriff's men who came to investigate refused to pursue the white man. One said, "What do you want me to do? Jump overboard after him?" The next day Taylor found hair matted with blood in the thorn tree.

Perez tried to place the blame for the arson attempts on "outside agitators." He wrote to a man in New Orleans who had offered financial assistance to a victim, "I have your letter commenting on the Belle Chasse negro church arson attempt. Our fire department, sheriff's office and safety engineer promptly took care of the situation, and investigation points to the fact that the attempted burning of this negro church was by some outside trouble makers, particularly CORE, who would like to stir up racial strife in the parish where peace and harmony prevail throughout. I personally saw the old negro preacher and told him that I would help take care of the damage to restore his church. . . . So while we appreciate your offer, the matter will be taken care of locally. Since you mentioned it, I will forward your $5.00 money order to the Wallace campaign."

The parish mobilized against the threatened influx of demonstrators and federal agents. The conversion of Fort St. Philip had brought nationwide attention to Plaquemines, although the prison had not been used; District Attorney Lea Perez, Jr., let it be known that the "mere presence" of civil rights workers in the parish was grounds for their arrest for disturbing the peace. Roadblocks often controlled access to the parish, and the ferries were closely watched. The Commission Council passed an ordinance requiring permission for public meetings of any kind.

"We're not near ready to surrender our peaceful, beautiful parish to the Communists," Perez announced. "And if Martin Luther King comes in, we'll guarantee his transportation across the river—part way, that is."

Plaquemines remained as it had been. In the Pointe a la Hache courthouse, signs designating "Colored" and "White" remained above rest rooms and drinking fountains; the ferries remained segregated, and some restaurants and clubs along the highways were clearly marked "For Negroes Only." Plaquemines seemed an obvious target for civil rights workers, but the parish's decentralized population, the absence of any large towns, the amount of land to be covered, and its relative inaccessibility made a concerted effort difficult. Also, there seemed to be disproportionate danger, and an uncommon amount of demoralization among black people in Plaquemines. A CORE worker who carried out clandestine missions in the parish reported that blacks walking on the sides of the roads "jump out of the way when they see a car coming, as if they're accustomed to being driven at." Rationalization by outside workers was common and understandable. "This isn't the kind of place you go into on a whim," said one official of CORE; another conceded that meetings with local blacks were difficult to arrange because of fear of reprisals. "Negroes in the parish are very secretive. They don't know whom to trust, so they trust no one."

Still, signs of movement began to appear—though they were extremely tentative. A *States-Item* reporter who managed to get into a meeting of a small group of blacks in Buras noted that the meeting convened with the playing of a scratchy recording of the song "Born Free." Those at the meeting "talked about how people outside the parish wanted to help them. The feeling was that hands were reaching over the wall."

CORE planned to send less than a dozen workers into the parish, to start voter registration and desegregation of public facilities. "We'll try to work as routinely as possible," said Richard Haley, the Southern regional director. "The other side should provide enough flamboyance for us all."

Plaquemines's Commissioner of Public Safety, Luke Petrovich, suggested that civil rights workers "will be a lot safer in the fort than they would be on the streets. People are going to say it's 'inhuman' or 'medieval' to use the fort, but we don't care." The white community seemed united behind Perez's announced resistance. One deputy sheriff told a reporter, "I've said many times that someday we'll be reading about the Judge in history books." A motel owner said, "Thanks to the Judge, every man in Plaquemines Parish can be a king if he wants to."

Steve Rubin, president of the American Civil Liberties Union Chapter in New Orleans, described Plaquemines as "probably the worst political unit in the country in terms of civil liberties and total domination by one man." His chief concern, if civil rights workers were thrown into Fort St. Philip, would be the difficulty of getting lawyers to their clients. "We won't be able to rent a boat or land a helicopter unless Mr. Perez wants us to."

As things turned out, it was the United States Government that began registering black voters in Plaquemines. The 1965 Voting Rights Act was passed, and federal registrars were sent into the parish. According to voting records of Louisiana's secretary of state, in February 1964, only 97 black voters were registered in Plaquemines, out of a black population of about 6,500. Examiners set up in the Buras post office one morning in early August, and Perez made no attempt to interfere; indeed, it didn't seem that interference was necessary, since for almost two hours no one showed up to register. Then, a stocky black man in a bright sport shirt entered the tiny office, emerged with a white registration slip, and quickly left the post office without giving his name to reporters. Then a black woman arrived, admitted that she was "a little shaky-like," and registered. Black people began to arrive regularly, and at one point there was a short line of prospective voters. An investigator for the district attorney showed up briefly with a tape recorder, and asked those in line their names and addresses, but there were no other signs of intimidation. A black man named Andrew Franklin told reporters after he had registered, "Nothing in God's world never scared me. . . . This is a brand new day in Plaquemines Parish. That parish registrar once told me I had to know the whole Constitution. I told him, 'How come I didn't have to know it when I fought for my country?' " He also said, "Negroes just can't get jobs in Plaquemines, not even cutting grass."

Some fifty blacks registered to vote that day; predictably, before the month was out Perez complained that unqualified parish residents were being registered. He based his argument on the technicality that in order to qualify, a resident had to be twenty-one years old and a resident of the parish for six months. If the person was not of age when the registration books closed thirty days before an election, but his birthday fell before December of that particular year, he could still be registered. Perez claimed people were being registered without regard to their date of birth. To no one's surprise, district judge Rudolph McBride issued a restraining order, temporarily halting the voter registration, although more than two thousand new voters had already been registered—most of those black. The district court's order was later dissolved in federal district court.

The Commission Council was also busy passing ordinances to stem the invasion. One ordinance required itinerant workers, or any workers coming in from outside Plaquemines, to be fingerprinted and photographed, and to carry with them an identification card which they were required to show to any police officer upon demand. The A.F.L.-C.I.O. brought suit against the constitutionality of the ordinance, and the Council amended it, requiring employers to keep a file on all outside employees. The Council also offered a reward of five hundred dollars for information leading to the conviction of anyone threatening or "compelling" Negroes to vote; however, apparently cognizant of increasing national attention, they also legislated a thousand dollar reward for information leading to the conviction of anyone burning Negro homes or churches.

The nationwide interest that focused on Plaquemines now brought various visitors to the parish. A group of students from Sarah Lawrence College showed up and asked for a tour of Fort St. Philip. Perez personally escorted them through the prison, explaining that it was to be used to discourage demonstrations "which amount to plain anarchy and are Communist-inspired." He added that according to a parish ordinance, demonstrators could be imprisoned for three days while an "investigation" was conducted, and could be held after that until bond was posted; it was all precautionary—in case "a dark cloud [should] drift over Plaquemines."

Firm in their admiration for his leadership in the face of "outside agitation," a local musical group eulogized Perez in song:

There's a man I know from my home town who's really
    very great.
I wish he were president of the whole United States.
He stays a step ahead of those who think they're
    smartest now,
But when they find just where they stand, it's just too
    wet to plow.
There'd be a White House cleaning, and you'd even dust
    the shelf.
You'd have the place as spotless as Mister Clean himself.
I'd like to hear you tell them off, just what they ought
    to know.
I've got a hunch you'd tell that bunch just where they
    could go.

*You'd catch 'em by their collars, and you'd sock 'em in
the nose.*
*You'd knock 'em down and beat 'em up, and hang 'em
by their toes.*
*And when they hollered that's enough, you'd cut 'em
down and then,*
*You'd turn around and stomp the ground, and do it once
again.*
You've got a place for all those who lots of trouble make,
A free ride in a cattle boat, and a bed behind the gate,
*Where the skeeters they are real vampires, and the
snakes just grow and grow,*
On this little isle of paradise, near the Gulf of Mexico.
Judge Perez, Judge Perez, I'm for you,
O'er the Stars and the Stripes and the Blue.
I know this great big nation needs some real intelligence.
I wish you were in Washington, and were our President.

In September of 1965, Hurricane Betsy drove up from the
Gulf, causing widespread damage along the coast and demol-
ishing many homes and buildings in Plaquemines. Water
pushed by the wind up the Mississippi topped the front levees,
and met even more flood waters moving in across the salt
marshes from the Gulf. When the water finally went down, the
parish was faced with a cleaning-up and rebuilding task of
massive proportions. The frequent intense storms that strike
the parish have always acted as major deterrents to unified
political opposition: the residents are preoccupied with personal disaster, and can hardly oppose those on whom they must
rely in times of crisis. Thus, hurricanes usually provide effective diversion. This time, however, the storm led indirectly to
an aggravation of Perez's problems.

A few days after the hurricane, the New Orleans office of
the F.B.I. received complaints that blacks in Plaquemines were
being forced at gunpoint to assist in clean-up operations. The
N.A.A.C.P. made specific complaints on behalf of two black
teachers, Clarence Marchand and Fred Patterson, who worked

at the Scottsville school. According to Marchand, "we were walking toward the cafeteria and were accosted by Leander Perez, Sr., and his bodyguard, known to me as 'Dutch.'* Perez said, 'Hey, Thomas [referring to the school janitor accompanying them], get me a bus and a driver.' And to Mr. Patterson and myself he said, 'You two damn boys get on the bus, you're going to work.' We tried to explain to him that we were teachers and had special duties to perform. He said, 'Damn what you have to do, get your asses on that bus.' Miss Andree Lawrence, our principal, came out of the academic building and tried to explain to him that we were teachers and that Mr. Moncla, the superintendent, had instructed us to perform other duties. He said, 'The hell with their duties. I'll take care of Moncla.'

"At this point his bodyguard said, 'All right, niggers, get the hell on the bus.' I refused, and he said, 'You'll get on, one way or another.' Again I refused. He grabbed my right arm and raised his club (a three-foot stick with an iron tip) to hit me. Mr. Patterson grabbed me and said, 'Let's get on the bus to prevent getting hurt.' When we were on the bus, Perez asked, 'Which one of you niggers started that trouble?' I said that I had started it. He said, 'Nigger, if you had hit Mr. Dutch, they would have had to take you away from here in an ambulance.' We were taken to the Boothville-Venice high school [all white] to clean up."

Patterson's statement was similar. He quoted Perez as saying, when the two men refused to board the bus, "I have two or three hundred of you niggers here in this school [as refugees from the hurricane], eating my food, and you're getting on this bus."

---

*Perez's bodyguard, Dutch Assavedo, was a special investigator for the district attorney's office. A short, extraordinarily sturdy Spaniard with a heavy jaw and a tight grin, he had a reputation as a man best not angered. He was devoted to the Judge, shared his belief in the Zionist conspiracy, and in later years accompanied him almost everywhere, carrying a .38 Magnum either on the seat of his car or inside his jacket. Dutch was said to have persuaded some blacks to help clean up the roads by wielding a submachine gun. Asked about this a few years later, he said, "I've had so many different guns in my hands so many times, that I can't remember what gun I was holding at any particular time."

The N.A.A.C.P. claimed that many Negroes had been forced to work at gunpoint, and explained that "a request was made for volunteer workers to clean the roads in Plaquemines Parish, with no one responding. Later on in the day, Mr. Leander Perez, Sr., was able to get sixty-five volunteers (volunteer is literal) to work on the roads."

Perez also rejected a plan of the American Red Cross to operate three emergency refugee centers in Plaquemines during the hurricane season because the plan didn't state whether the centers would be segregated.

The F.B.I. turned the N.A.A.C.P.'s complaints over to the Justice Department, and intervention by the federal government in the Twenty-fifth Judicial District seemed inevitable; in the next election, federal observers descended upon six parishes in southern Louisiana, including Plaquemines and St. Bernard. Perez blasted the observers as "spies" and "enemies." When he made his traditional round of the polling places—accompanied by Mama Perez, who seemed determined to keep Lélé from clashing openly with representatives of the federal government—Perez discovered two observers at the Belle Chasse firehouse, one sitting at a table near the commissioners checking voters' names, and the other sitting at the back of the station. He pointed at the observer seated at the table, and told a *Times-Picayune* photographer, "Take a picture of that federal spy."

The observer seated at the back of the station came forward and said, "I don't believe I know you."

"No, you don't know me," Perez told him, "and you're not going to know me."

He walked over to the table and instructed the voting commissioners, "If these federal observers get in your way, tell them to get out of here."

One of the observers said, "If you're telling us to go, we'll go."

Perez seemed aware of what further trouble *that* might lead to. "I didn't say any such thing," he shouted. "You know that, you smart aleck."

Perez stormed out of the firehouse, followed by Mama. He wanted to go to the polls across the river at Braithwaite, but the ferry had already left. Perez ordered someone to telephone the captain and tell him to come back and pick them up. The ferry was in the middle of a scheduled crossing, loaded with cars and passengers, but when the captain received the call, he wheeled the big craft around in the middle of the Mississippi and returned for the Judge.

Perez told reporters accompanying him, "I want these commissioners to know they're not to trust these federal people. They are our enemies." He added that he didn't expect any trouble. "Those federal people would like to use Plaquemines Parish, but they're not."

Outside the auditorium in Braithwaite, a man approached Perez and told him in hushed tones that one of the federal observers inside had asked Perez's daughter-in-law—a voting commissioner—if she was "Spanish." Perez hurried inside, and demanded of the observers seated at the commissioners' table, "Which one of you federal spies asked my daughter-in-law if she's Spanish?"

The two observers looked at each other; the man who had asked the question identified himself.

"You've got no right to talk to our ladies that way," Perez told him. "I don't want to hear tell of you spies talking to our ladies at all, you understand?"

"You've got my word, sir," the man said, and he went on to explain that he was himself of Spanish descent.

"You must be Spanish," Perez said. "You think you're cute." He turned to the commissioners. "I want to caution you to be wary of these federal spies. Just because they smile at you and try to strike up a conversation, they're here to watch you and they would stick a stake in your breast. This is the second Reconstruction. I can tell you, it's going to get a lot worse. These spies have no damn business at this table. Don't treat them like decent Americans. They'd like it, but don't do it."

He then signed the register, stepped into the voting machine, and voted. When he came out, he noticed drinking cups on the table in front of the observers. He picked up one cup and threw it across the room. "Don't give them a glass of water or a crumb of bread," he said. "Treat them as federal spies."

He stomped out of the auditorium.

Federal observers were not the worst thing Perez had to face. His refusal to desegregate Plaquemines's public schools cost the parish approximately $200,000 in federal aid in 1965. The following summer the Justice Department filed suit in federal district court to have Plaquemines ordered to desegregate. Presiding was Judge Herbert Christenberry, who during initial hearings listened to Justice Department lawyers and to Perez and his son Chalin, representing the parish. The Justice Department pointed out that no blacks attended school with whites in the parish, except in the "French-Indian" community of Grand Bayou, a remote area where thirty-eight children of various races and national origins attended classes together. In the parish's eight other public schools, there was no mixing.

Perez and Chalin did not deny the charge. Instead, they sought to show that Plaquemines's "happy way of life" was common to all residents, and the result of good leadership. Perez even had his Commissioner of Public Safety, Luke Petrovich, say, "I know it sounds trite, but Judge Perez is regarded as the father of his people." He added that Plaquemines residents were the best-informed people in the world. "The Judge fills them in on everything," Petrovich said. To make sure no one missed the point, Perez asked Petrovich, "Have the people faith in Judge Perez as a man of integrity and principle?" Petrovich said, "Yes, sir."

The government produced witnesses who had signed statements saying they wanted their children to attend a school that had been traditionally white. Mrs. Alberta Anderson, a black mother of ten, testified that a representative of the school board came to her home one night after she had signed the statement, and asked why she wanted her children to attend the all-white Woodlawn School. She stated that she had changed her mind that very night when the school board member told her he "didn't know what would happen" if she didn't.

Moncla, Plaquemines's school superintendent, testified that the school board had signed all its property over to the Commission Council and that therefore the schools came under the Council's jurisdiction. He added that the school board had been planning such a move for five years, and had just happened to go through with it a month before. Judge Christenberry called Moncla's claim "ridiculous" and issued a restraining order on the property transfer.

Perez stood up before the packed courtroom and accused Christenberry of deciding the case in advance, and of disrupting his presentation of "evidence." Christenberry threatened Perez with contempt, and told him, "If it weren't for your age, and if I didn't know you so well, you might be held in contempt and might go to jail." He added that the Perezes' defense was "the most disorderly case I've ever seen presented."

He rejected Perez's attack on the Fourteenth Amendment, and ordered Plaquemines's schools desegregated.

The Shreveport *Times* commented editorially with what in a less reactionary publication might have been satire: "Perez . . . included in his brief the matter-of-fact assertion that . . . no Negroes *want* to integrate. That's a little more like it. Considering Mr. Perez's hold on Plaquemines Parish, he may have polled the population down there and discovered to nobody's surprise that everybody is happy. It's just like the federal prosecutors, though, to spoil such idyllic situations by introducing contrary evidence."

Perez raged against the federal government for playing "dirty politics," and promised with a characteristically mixed metaphor "to fight to the last ditch, come hell or high water." He denounced Christenberry's order as "criminal and Communistic" and a "gag rule." He attempted to get a new trial of the Justice Department's suit, and a delay in the desegregation order, but Christenberry refused, saying, "It's been twelve years. If we had a situation here where we might expect or-

derly legal compliance in, say, six months, then I might post-
pone the order. But there is no reason in the world to believe
that there will ever be voluntary compliance with the law in
Plaquemines Parish."

In September, Perez appeared on television denouncing the
Supreme Court's desegregation rulings as being based upon
"Communist writings," and claiming that "back of it all is the
destruction of our institutions, . . . hundreds of thousands of
our white youths have been driven out of our public school
system. . . . What will be the situation in the United States in
the next two or three generations? . . . Where will the army of
industrial workers . . . come from to maintain the might of the
United States, which might comes from our industrial empire?
Where will the technologists . . . come from, when the hundreds of thousands of our white youths are being driven [out]
by the federal government, doing the work of the Communist-
like traitors?"

Christenberry's order stipulated that enrollment levels in
Plaquemines's schools should not fall substantially below what
they were the previous year—an attempt to prevent a mass
exodus of white pupils to the private schools being hastily set
up in Plaquemines. When Perez was asked how the new private schools would function under this order, he said, "How
can the superman from the bench say that parents have to send
their children to school, whether they want to or not?" He said
the people of Plaquemines had demonstrated their resource-
fulness by removing most of the scars left by hurricane Betsy
(with the institution of "voluntary" labor), but "the scar of this
damnable Communist order goes deeper and does more harm.
. . . The Negroes and white people in our parish have always
been on the friendliest of terms. But I don't say that our people
will take it lying down. It's up to them. . . . What we do
depends upon the people—but no damn court. No rotten
Communist-driven politicians can force our people to do what
they don't want. . . . Our people are peaceful. I'd say, taken
over-all, they are high class. . . . I know that Lyndon Johnson
and Katzenbach couldn't let Martin Luther King down, or

CORE or the NAACP. No, he's looking for the consensus, but damn Lyndon's hide, he will see that the consensus in this country will turn against him just because he is going along with the Communist plan and controlled race riots. They are not Democrats—they are Mob-ocrats!"

Perez used the Plaquemines *Gazette* to admonish his people. He told them that their schools had been "confiscated" by the federal government "for control of the Communist bloc vote. . . . Proof? Remember Little Rock when so many citizens received bloody heads from bayonets? Or Oxford, Mississippi, where college students were brutalized and put into tear gas chambers?"

The *Gazette* also ran Perez's "Fourteenth Amendment Treatise" in which he sought to prove that the amendment had never really been ratified. It was printed in serial form, and readers were advised, "Since . . . it is a comprehensive and vital document, it is suggested that readers clip the installments out of the paper each week in order to have a complete treatise for reference."

Desegregation finally came to Plaquemines's schools without violence. It had been expected for some time, and much of the potential fury was probably spent in Perez's public statements; more important, he, school officials, and the Commission Council proposed a two million dollar private school system for white children, and set up the first "academy" at Promised Land, Perez's home in the days before he moved his official residence to the west bank of the river. When 5 black pupils entered Woodlawn School, 250 white pupils switched to Promised Land. Woodlawn teachers and bus drivers boycotted the school, and the lunch program was discontinued.

Other public schools in Plaquemines were desegregated, and though attendance fell off by half, they remained open. Three other private schools eventually opened to handle the children of those parents in the parish either actively opposed to desegregation or concerned about their continuing position in parish affairs, as well as the children of some families outside the parish who were strongly opposed to desegregation. St. Bernard schools were also desegregated, after some minor incidents and intimidation, but the percentage of blacks in St. Bernard's population was quite small. Many families fled New Orleans to live in St. Bernard for this reason, and this burgeoning new population, though mostly committed to Perez's racial stand, eventually cut into his influence in St. Bernard.

Plaquemines's private schools existed with the aid of contributions from some industries operating in the parish, tuition paid by the parents of students, and a "scholarship" system with which parish funds were used to aid families unable to pay the full tuition. An ordinance was passed whereby public transportation—i.e., school buses—could be used to transport private-school children for free. These same pupils were also given jobs in the parish—for instance, cutting grass along the highways—that had once been given to blacks; their earnings helped support the private schools.

The federal government kept a close eye on Plaquemines. The court later ordered that black students be allowed to participate on an equal basis in extracurricular activities, which Perez said included "drama, variety shows and *dances*! . . . We say that our white girls will not be used as political pawns to dance with or to be embraced by Negroes." He told a group of segregationist parents in Port Sulphur that "politics is a dirty game, and your children are the pawns in that dirty game. . . . Make up your minds to stand together in the next presidential election. If the people of the six Southern states used as whipping boys for the radical liberal bloc votes in the Northern and Eastern states . . . would vote solidly for presidential electors for George Wallace . . . then the South could hold the balance of power and restore constitutional government in this country."

It was not the last time he would make this appeal. Perez had lost the battle with the federal government on the local level, but those defeats only seemed to strengthen his denunciations and his contempt for his enemies. He didn't seem to realize that he was becoming an anachronistic, slightly pathetic figure, perhaps because die-hard segregationists all over the South continued to regard him as the symbol of resistance. When Lurleen Wallace ran for governor of Alabama in 1966, Perez contributed to the campaign, and received a letter from George Wallace himself thanking Perez for his "generous" contribution.

Perez also wrote to Lester Maddox congratulating him on his primary victories in Georgia, and instructed Maddox "to remind Georgia voters that several Southern states supported Eisenhower and all they got out of his election was the Civil Rights Commission, Earl Warren, the Black Monday decision . . . and the 101st Airborne Division in Little Rock, which set the pattern for using the military to enforce the unlawful integration orders by the federal courts. I enclose a contribution to help you in your good work."

Perez hated Lyndon Johnson, and once claimed that Johnson "joined in the international hymn of hate, 'We Shall Overcome,' with five black-robed U.S. Supreme Court judges clapping in rhythm and, in effect, supporting armed rebellion and violence throughout this country." But he also opposed Republicans in general after the Goldwater debacle and his run-in with Everett Dirksen, and specifically opposed Richard Nixon, whom he described as a "Leftist."

Perez was awarded a plaque for his segregationist efforts by the New Orleans Citizens Council. Ned Touchstone, editor of the *Councilor*, delivered a tribute which the Plaquemines *Gazette* ran under the banner headline "JUDGE PEREZ CITED AS GREATEST HERO OF MODERN TIMES." Touchstone mourned the passing of "those patriots who had shown the courage of [Joseph] McCarthy . . . and others who had dared to speak out against the Red conspiracy. One by one, those Old Grey Eagles have flown from this perch to claim a higher reward. . . . Off yonder where the Mississippi River twists its way to the sea, there is yet one of those old grey eagles with the courage to speak out. Leander Perez Lives! . . . His courage is even now a beacon light for younger eagles who take heart, and will rise soon to reclaim the glory of America. . . . We salute Leander

Perez, a man who knows a worm when he sees one. A man who can scorn the pettiness of Martin Luther King, Emanuel Celler, Ladybird's fling and Nelson Rockefeller. . . . Neither Pink Judge nor Red Priest, neither civil rights leader nor corrupt politician, has been able to stay the hands or honest words of this man we salute. Tonight we walk where history is made. We want you to know, Leander Perez, that your secret is out— your honesty and your heart are known to these people."

Behind the Marsh Curtain

*The closer you keep government to the
people, the more democracy you have.*

Leander Perez

The Judge and Mama Perez were planning to celebrate their fiftieth wedding anniversary in 1967, but early in the year she died of a heart attack in her daughter's New Orleans home. She had just been released from a stay in the Baptist Hospital, and she and Perez were talking when the attack occurred. She was seventy-one, four years younger than her husband, and the grandmother of nineteen. Six of the grandchildren served as pallbearers at the funeral, which was held at the Holy Name of Jesus Church on the Loyola University campus. (It was commonly known that she had been unable, as he had, to accept his excommunication as just a political setback.) Perez was solemn but in control throughout the ceremony, though he was greatly affected by his wife's death, and never got over the loss. Mama Perez was buried at Metairie Cemetery, but soon afterward Perez had a brick mausoleum built behind his home at Idlewild, shaded by oaks hung with Spanish moss, and had his wife's body transferred there. The mausoleum contained room enough for more than one casket.

About this time, the Judge faced a resurgence of opposition at home. He decided that it was time for his son Chalin to become president of the Commission Council (Lea seemed satisfied with the perennial district-attorneyship), and Chalin announced his candidacy for Commissioner of Public Affairs in the upcoming election. At the same time, the Plaquemines Independent Democratic Organization, a small opposition group founded in the late 1950's which had ineffectively fielded a few candidates in each election, announced that Ernest Hingle would oppose Chalin. Hingle had been associated with the anti faction in the southern half of the parish for thirty years, and had run for numerous offices. "Every time I tried to qualify for something," he said, "I got sued. Once I was charged with arson, and on election day I had to go to the courthouse to find out what I was supposed to have burned down." In the 1959 election, the Independents had run Emile Martin III, a local lawyer, for state representative, and Ben Slater, who had been Perez's ally in Louisiana's Little War but was later dropped by the organization, for sheriff. Perez was enraged by the fact that these candidates managed to qualify; a witness at the Belle Chasse polling place on election day said that Perez drove up, saw Martin on the side of the road, and drove directly toward him. Mama Perez grabbed the steering wheel, and the car just missed striking Martin. Perez then got out of the car, walked up to Slater and slapped a cigar out of his mouth. Slater seemed grateful that retribution had ended there.

So in 1967 the Independents knew that they would not be welcomed by the local Democratic executive committee. In addition to Hingle, the Independents planned to run candidates for sheriff, clerk of court, state representative, and state senator. They soon discovered that qualifying as candidates was no easier for antis than it had ever been. The Democratic executive committee met as was required, but minutes of the meeting could not be found posted in the courthouse. Potential candidates were unable to discover either the deadline for qualification or the required fees.

Hingle decided to file his qualification papers at the executive committee headquarters—which appeared to be none other than Judge Perez's home. He wisely took some Indepen-

168

dents along as witnesses. Perez could hardly refuse the papers, but he gave all the Independents a lecture about what he considered to be their motives for opposing the ruling clique. "I know what you're trying to do," Perez said. "You're trying to get your hands on the money. Well, you'll never do it."

One of the witnesses was a contractor named Lawrence Rousselle, who had worked for the Independents in the past, mostly helping organize and passing out campaign literature at the polls. Rousselle was born in Potash, in southern Plaquemines, and now lived in Belle Chasse; he didn't consider himself particularly "political" and wasn't running for office, but he was opposed on principle to the Perez machine and its methods. He had built a laundromat on the highway in Belle Chasse, and then discovered that he couldn't get a permit to expand; gas supplied to the building was periodically shut off without explanation, and he often discovered out-of-order signs hanging on functioning washing machines. Rousselle had been particularly outspoken about this type of harassment, and as he and the other Independents were leaving Perez's home, the Judge told Rousselle, "I'll shut you up, one way or another."

That evening Rousselle stopped at a gas station near his home. Several men were talking together, and Rousselle joined them; when the conversation switched to Judge Perez, as it usually did in Plaquemines, Rousselle told some stories of Perez's past exploits, including the story about the trappers who came after Perez with guns. Rousselle said, "It's a wonder he's lived as long as he has."

Rousselle returned to his home, a bungalow on a Belle Chasse back street where he lived with his wife Shirley and his four children, and which he was in the process of renovating. The family had supper and went to bed; around midnight, Rousselle was awakened by someone pounding on the front door. He went downstairs and opened the door, confronting two armed deputies. Two patrol cars waited in the street, containing another deputy and a police dog. The deputies at the door told Rousselle that he was under arrest for conspiracy to commit murder, pushed their way into his house, and followed him back to his bedroom, where they watched him dress.

Rousselle's wife was badly frightened, and he was convinced he was going to be killed. "They took me out and put me in the back seat of one of the cars, all by myself, and they didn't even lock the doors. They drove down the highway real slow, the other car following with the headlights out. They wanted me to cut and run, so they could shoot me, and I was so scared I almost did run."

At the Pointe a la Hache jail, Rousselle was placed in a six-by-nine-foot cell with no light; he was not allowed to make a telephone call. Judge Eugene Leon, Perez's man on the local bench, told Rousselle that he might get eleven years at hard labor for his crime, but would not tell him whose murder he was supposed to have plotted, and then set his bond at $75,000. Rousselle spent three days and nights in that cell, before he was allowed out to shave and to see his wife. He was then placed in another cell, this time one with a light; it burned twenty-four hours a day.

In the meantime, Richard Dowling had been contacted by Rousselle's wife and was attempting to get the bond lowered and Rousselle released. Dowling, a well-known lawyer and an old anti, had been defeated in his bid for a second term as New Orleans district attorney by a relatively unknown lawyer named Jim Garrison, who had received substantial backing from Perez. (Garrison later wrote to Perez expressing his gratitude, and offering to help the Judge or Lea Perez any time they needed his services.) Dowling was unable to discover who it was that was supposed to be murdered, how or where the murder was supposed to have taken place, or who the alleged co-conspirators were.

Hingle and the other Independents charged Perez with political retaliation against Rousselle, a charge Perez branded "a damn lie. . . . I understand there was a group of s.o.b.'s who raised $25,000 to murder me." He told a reporter that Rousselle "came here with Hingle and I told him I heard he was using my name in vain and slandering me, and I told him the next time I saw him in public I would slap his face."

Perez then claimed that the "conspiracy" grew out of his own order, delivered more than a year before, to have ninety-six slot machines taken from a warehouse and dumped into the Mississippi. The machines, he said, were worth about $500,000, and he "understood" that the conspirators would be given the slot machine concession by outside forces—i.e., organized crime. The charge was generally dismissed as phony, an impression strengthened by Perez himself when he refused to name the alleged conspirators and said, "draw your own conclusions."

Lea Perez, apparently uninformed about the conspiracy, first said the idea was ridiculous. He later amended that statement, claiming that he had been misquoted by the newspapers, and added gravely, "This does not involve politics in any way. It gets out of the realm of something that's amusing when there is a plot to kill a man. Particularly your father."

Dowling, unable to learn the official charge against his client from either the district attorney or the Plaquemines sheriff's office, made a verbal plea before the state supreme court. A reduction of the bail from $75,000 to $10,000 was granted, and Rousselle was finally released—after spending a total of nineteen days in jail on a charge that could never even be specifically determined by his own attorney.

Rousselle promptly addressed a group of Independents in Port Sulphur, telling them, "I can't stand confinement, but I did a lot of thinking while I was in jail. . . . I've never liked politics, but I decided in there that I was going to get involved. I'm going to get this man [Perez], and I don't mean kill him. We'll get him at the ballot box." Then, close to tears, Rousselle said, "I've accepted the fact that I'm going to lose a sixty thousand dollar building that I built with my own hands because that man is going to keep me from opening for business because I talk too much."

Hingle returned to Perez's home, this time accompanied by Angelo Benandi, the owner of a small produce company who wanted to run for clerk of court, and Thomas McBride, who wished to run for the state senate. It was a weekday morning;

the trio walked around to the back door of Perez's home, where they had been received before, and Hingle knocked. Perez shouted, "Stay outside. I'll be with you in a while."

They waited a few minutes, but Perez didn't appear. They knocked again, and Perez came out, accompanied by his bodyguard, Assavedo. He asked McBride, "What are these two damn fellows doing here with you?"

McBride said they were there as witnesses to the filing of his qualification papers; Perez said he needed "no damn witnesses" and that to bring them was an insult. Benandi spoke up, saying that the minutes of the Democratic executive committee meeting had not been posted in the courthouse. Perez called him a "damn liar." Hingle said he wasn't lying, because he had personally searched the courthouse and couldn't find the minutes. Hingle later recalled what happened:

"The Judge was sitting down, and this [conversation] seemed to irritate him very much. He then proceeded to jump up, and stated that 'you both are a goddamn nuisance, and I'm now declaring this property off-limits to you. This is my private property.' We still stood there and listened to him, and when we didn't move, he riled up and told his bodyguard, Dutch, 'Get these goddamn fellows out of here. I don't want them to set foot on this property again.'"

Dutch dutifully accompanied the men to their car.

Rousselle's troubles were far from over. One night he received a telephone call from an unidentified woman who told him that a horse he grazed on the levee near his home was running loose. He got into his car and drove to the levee, a pistol on the seat beside him; he saw the horse tied where he had left it, and another car parked near some underbrush. "I could see four or five men inside," Rousselle later recalled. "They drove ahead of me, back to the road, then they stopped and got out, and one of them came up and said, 'Nobody's going to tail-gate me.' So I just picked up that pistol. The others came up and tried to joke about it. . . . They drove off, and went straight to a political rally in Belle Chasse, where the Judge was."

Rousselle was arrested and charged with aggravated assault; this time he spent only five days in jail, although he was never brought to trial and the charges were left pending—a standard Perez ploy. "I realized they were just trying to shake me," he said, "and I wasn't going to let them." Rousselle later filed suit in federal district court in New Orleans, seeking damages of $150,000 from Perez, Judge Leon, and the deputies who had arrested him on the conspiracy charge.

Perez and the courthouse clique received some opposition from another quarter also. A Washington lawyer named Richard Sobol, chief staff counsel for the Lawyers Constitutional Defense Committee, ventured into Plaquemines to represent a young black charged with battery for allegedly slapping a white youth on the arm. When Sobol returned to the parish alone two months later to get an appeal bond signed for his client, he was arrested and charged with practicing law without a license. Various out-of-state lawyers working for civil rights in the South had run into harassment and legal trouble, but Sobol was the first actually to wind up in court for unauthorized law practice. He was twenty-nine years old, third in his law class at Columbia, and had belonged to the prestigious firm of Arnold, Fortas and Porter before coming South, having been "struck by the tremendous impact one well-educated lawyer, working full time, could have on the field of civil rights."

Sobol's case was handled by Alvin Bronstein, former chief staff counsel for the Lawyers Constitutional Defense Committee. The prosecution was enjoined and the case quickly moved to federal court, where a three-judge panel sat through ten days of hearings. Sobol, Bronstein, and another attorney, Anthony Amsterdam, wanted the prosecution permanently enjoined, and the Louisiana statutes regulating the practice of law declared unconstitutional insofar as they applied to out-of-state lawyers. They claimed that Sobol's client, Gary Duncan, had a right to counsel of his own choice, that existing statutes were "vague and over-broad," and that there weren't enough Louisiana lawyers willing to defend blacks in civil rights cases.

During the course of the hearings, an array of witnesses were produced who testified that they couldn't find local white attorneys to represent them; Bronstein was also empowered to take depositions from Perez; in doing so, Bronstein attempted to reveal the extent of Perez's influence in Plaquemines, and how the parish actually operated.

The depositions were taken in the middle of August 1967, in the Maritime Building in New Orleans; the court reporter was asked by Bronstein to record everything said in the confrontation. Perez appeared with a large cigar in his mouth, accompanied by his attorney, S. W. Provensal, and by Judge Leon and Lea Perez, Jr. When Bronstein introduced himself and Sobol, Perez said, "I'd like to see the names written out, because Soboloff and Bronstein, it sounds like Russian to me."

Bronstein established that Perez—who was required by the court to answer pertinent questions about himself—was the chairman of various local Democratic executive committees, legal adviser to the levee board, a stockholder in the Delta Bank and Trust Company, Plaquemines's only bank, and author of the constitutional amendment enabling Plaquemines to change its form of government. Perez admitted, "I have written hundreds of bills for members of the Legislature. I have been their unofficial adviser, as it was, because of my acquaintances with some members, and my friendship with them and their confidence in me as an attorney."

When Bronstein asked about the parish ordinance requiring the fingerprinting of itinerant workers, Perez said, "There were a number of undesirable characters and criminals who drifted into the parish . . . and I dictated that ordinance . . . and within two weeks there was a pack of rats and criminals leaving the parish. It was noble."

Perez maintained his testiness. At one point he told Bronstein a question "didn't have a darn thing to do with the case." He told the reporter, "Don't take all that rubbish down," referring to incidental conversation about Perez's desire for another cigar. When Bronstein used the word "expertise," Perez instructed him, "I don't like that word. I've seen it used federally." Asked a hypothetical question about out-of-state lawyers coming into Plaquemines, Perez said, "If you are a member, for instance, of the American Civil Liberties League [sic] or of any other Communist organization . . . we would make it very inconvenient for you. . . . We don't welcome that kind of trash, or rats and law violators who would destroy our system of government. . . . I personally, not as president of the Council, but as a man, if I saw him agitating unthinking Negroes to disturb the peace, I'd handle him personally, as a man. . . . We will protect the peace and good order of our community. And we fortunately haven't had anybody to try and disturb it yet. Now, if you want to try your luck, Mr. Sobol, if that's the type of a character you are, you try it."

Bronstein said, "I'm Mr. Bronstein."

"I don't know," Perez said. "You look like Sobol. Who is Sobol?"

Asked about Fort St. Philip, Perez said it was intended to house civil rights demonstrators who were "simply tools of Communist agitators . . . which strive for national disunity, and they have succeeded beyond their fondest dreams to extend an armed rebellion and destruction of billions of dollars of property with Molotov bombs and shooting of police and firemen in the back."

At one point Perez demanded that the air conditioner be turned off, and it was, though he continued to fill the room with cigar smoke. Bronstein later recalled, "It never occurred to anyone to object, although it was hot and stuffy in the room. He was a very authoritative man. When he asked for another cigar, I found myself patting my pockets to see if I had one to offer. . . . During the entire time he never took his eyes off mine, and I had the weird sensation that he could actually see my brain working."

Perez admitted threatening to transport Martin Luther King "part way" across the river if he came to Plaquemines, but added that it depended upon "his conduct on the way. . . . Hey, are you defending Martin Luther King? Is he one of your idols?"

About blacks, Perez said, "Negroes generally are immoral. I know that a large number . . . have illegitimate children. . . . I might add that I'm not anti-Negro. I'm anti-Communist, and I'm against the Communists using the Negroes for their purposes. And that's proven all over the country."

Asked about his influence outside of Plaquemines, Perez said, "I've helped to elect quite a few judges. But I never take credit for anything I do. I let it go by, whatever I do as a matter of public service, and I forget about it. I never remind anyone that I helped elect him, whether he is the governor or a judge of the [state] Supreme Court or the court of appeals or anybody else. I do it in the public interest, nothing personal."

Perez objected often to Bronstein's wide range of questions. He told the lawyer, "with a mind as pigmented as yours, and as limited, and with the ideologies that undoubtedly you have, I'm impressed that it's not the proper legal principles." A question about the case of Lawrence Rousselle particularly upset Perez, who claimed that he had had nothing to do with the case.

"I would have confronted Rousselle and handled it myself as a man. But I yielded, let the law take its course." He claimed that his son Lea, the district attorney, had mentioned the conspiracy to him; "I said, 'You leave Rousselle to me.' And he said, 'That's just what I was afraid you'd say, so we'll have to proceed.' . . . Leave it to me, that's what I meant. And if Rousselle had admitted to me, personally, that he was in a conspiracy to murder me, Mr. Rousselle, well, I would have—do you know Rousselle?"

Bronstein said he did not.

"It's a matter of self-preservation," Perez told him. "You try it and you'll see what happens."

As they were getting up to leave the room after the session, Bronstein thanked the still highly indignant Perez, who responded, "Don't thank me. I'm not thanking you."

"Your manners, sir," said Bronstein, "are no concern of mine."

"What?"

176

Bronstein repeated the statement, and Perez asked, "You're not questioning my manners, are you? Don't get personal. Are you?"

Provensal hurriedly told Perez, "Judge, he's not questioning your manners. He knows better than that."

"I guess he does," Perez conceded, squaring his shoulders to leave the room. "That's one thing I demand, respect."

The federal judges eventually enjoined the prosecution of Sobol. A few years later, Sobol said of Perez: "He was very up-front with his racism, you knew where he stood. If I had to be stranded on a desert island with Perez or, say, the president of International Telephone and Telegraph, I'd pick Perez. . . . The political middle in America needs people like Perez to point to, to detract attention from its own deviousness."

Hingle and the other Independents were defeated in the Plaquemines election, but remained in opposition. Some joined the Parent-Teachers Associations of various public schools in the parish, and were instrumental in preventing a mass exodus of white children and the closing of the schools. An underground newssheet appeared, with no masthead and only a post office box for a mailing address. It was called the Plaquemines *Voice*, and an early mimeographed edition was headlined "Inside Plaquemines Parish or 'Behind the Marsh Curtain.'" The paper said, "An expression heard in Plaquemines Parish, all too often, is, 'If you don't like what goes on here, why don't you leave?' For the benefit of those who believe this misguided philosophy, we would like to remind them that geographically Plaquemines Parish is located within the boundaries of the United States. . . . The public school is the only institution which provides an environment in which the children of people who differ widely in religious, political, social and economic beliefs can come together in a spirit of mutual respect, acceptance and understanding. With [such] an educative process . . . dictatorship or dynasty cannot survive. . . . Much is said and done in Plaquemines Parish in the name of 'Americanism' and 'patriotism' . . . yet we have seen censorship of our reading in our public libraries, a monopolized press, and attempted control of religions, plus past complete control of our schools."

Chalin Perez, age forty-four, took office as Commissioner of Public Affairs, and was immediately elected president of the Commission Council by the other members. Luke Petrovich said, "It may seem extraordinary to have a new member become president, but Chalin is not new in public service."

Judge Perez, in relinquishing the office of president of the Council, cited the parish's achievements, and said that "the states have lost their most precious power—police power—to the federal government. In the days ahead, I will address myself to restoring Constitutional government to the nation. We must awaken the South to form a solid bloc and elect enough independent electors to throw the 1968 election into the House of Representatives. Then you'll see a change in government."

The Plaquemines *Gazette* reported the formal transferral of power from father to son with typical bromides: "A vast legacy of good government and a phenomenal public improvement program was handed down by Judge Perez. . . . He not only left the heritage of a Charter form of government . . . but he gave to the parish his own sons to carry on the work. . . . [The Judge's] eyes were moist . . . but his heart gratified that he was able to realize the fruition of his plan." He told the Council and a large audience of Plaquemines's residents, "I have no regrets for my career. If I had it to do over again, I would do it willingly." He scanned the room, and added, "It looks like people are happy here."

People laughed, and someone joked, "Maybe they're glad to see you go."

The Judge answered with a light, only slightly mixed metaphor: "I'll just roll with the blow, and take it in my stride."

A reception was held at the Community Center after the power transfer. A large cake in the center of the table was inscribed "L. H. Perez Sr., 1919–1967; Chalin O. Perez, 1967–?"

Chapter Seven

The Bequest

Mine is the life story of a man who's done more, I believe, than any other man in this country in a restricted area, in building up a community.

Leander Perez

The Great Father Looks Away

Officially unburdened of local affairs, Perez in 1968 could devote himself to sabotaging the 1968 presidential election. The year before, he had written to Lester Maddox that "the South has been made the whipping boy for the national Democratic administration, aided and abetted by leaders of the national Republican Party. . . . All signs point to a close presidential electoral election come November 1968. This should offer us an opportunity to get together without delay and plan for organization to restore the solid South to recover what we have lost." Perez invited Maddox and other Southern leaders to a meeting in New Orleans with George Wallace. Perez personally contributed at least five thousand dollars to the campaign, and felt entitled to give Wallace advice on various subjects. Once he wrote the Alabaman, "I believe the news media misquoted you as having said recently that you refused to follow the HEW guidelines [for desegregation] but that you would obey and carry out court orders. Of course, the court orders, under direction from Washington, adopted the HEW guidelines. . . . I sincerely hope that you will take every advantage of the opportunity . . . and express to the people of your state and the country the type of judicial tyranny practiced under presidential orders for absolute regimentation of our children which, in the final analysis, is nothing more nor less than 'Communism in the raw.' "

Perez planned another campaign to capture Louisiana for Wallace. When he discovered that Governor McKeithen would not back such a move, Perez urged his friends and members of the Citizens Councils to write to their governor "because he's slipping too far to the left. I think we can help him see the light of day." He urged support of Wallace on every level of state government, including the Plaquemines courthouse. The underground Plaquemines *Voice* printed a letter from a worker on the parish payroll that said, "If you work for the parish, are you a free man? Ask anybody who works for the parish. You get low pay and you gotta put up for everything, schools, Wallace, [segregated] swimming pools and anything Perez wants."

But Perez's greatest concern was the state Democratic Central Committee, where he still enjoyed the support of rural legislators and members he had helped elect. He often received letters like the one from a lobbyist, also addressed to Chalin, that read, "I've done quite a lot of traveling since we last met in an effort to help our friends. Success has varied across the state. Rather than write a book about how our candidates are doing, I'll simply pass along money needs." Perez was then asked for more than fifteen thousand dollars for the election of eight state legislators.

Perez had written a bill passed by the legislature that added twelve seats to the Central Committee and considerably strengthened the segregationist element. The legislature was already under court order to reapportion itself and shift voting strength to the more populous urban parishes, but Perez claimed that the Committee was under no such obligation. The election of Committee members had previously been based on representative districts, but Perez's bill assured every parish of one representative, even though there might have been as many as three parishes in one district. The reason he pushed the bill was that the twelve new representatives all came from conservative rural parishes.

The Judge also played a large part in the official numbering of representative districts; predictably, Plaquemines headed the list. "That showed how cunning and astute he was," said

DeBlieux, leader of the Committee's loyalist forces. "Perez could indicate in a roll call vote right off the bat where he stood on any issue, and his followers would then vote the same way. Perez would wait until the last minute to file his resolutions, and we wouldn't really get a chance to study them before the voting started."

The preferential primary placed Wallace on the general election ballot. Since the parties appeared on the ballot in alphabetical order, Wallace's American party came first. Perez attempted yet again to capture the rooster for Wallace, claiming that it was still the symbol of the state Democrats, and that the national Democrats should be forced to display a picture of a donkey on their ballot. That motion passed the committee, but the district court in Baton Rouge ruled against it. Perez appealed to the state supreme court.

In the meantime, he campaigned hard for Wallace, who wrote to Perez early in 1968, "It is particularly gratifying to know that you are willing to give your time and talents in behalf of our efforts. I am indeed grateful. . . . I hope that you will find time in your busy schedule to follow through in your state in the manner outlined in our discussions. . . . I am confident that as a team our efforts will be successful."

Perez told a rally in New Orleans that Wallace would restore "honesty in government. . . . It is time for law and order, and all it takes to get these things is determination, guts and will power. And George Wallace has the courage to accomplish this." He traveled around the South speaking in Wallace's behalf, and in Atlanta joined John Bell Williams and Maddox, who said the nation was "fed up . . . with snotty-nosed, stringy-haired, red-eyed, LSD-taking young'ns who range in age and IQ from 13 to 80." Perez told the gathering that the Democrats and Republicans would lead the nation into socialism. In June, Wallace wrote to Perez to thank him: "It is people like you who will help us carry this campaign forward to the millions of American people who desire a change in our system." One week before the election, Perez wrote to Wallace, "I enclose check for $30,000 to cover net receipts for our New Orleans

Wallace Testimonial Dinner. . . . Best wishes for a successful climax."

The state supreme court ruled in Perez's favor, and the American party received the emblem of the rooster for its ballots. But it was a narrow, spoiler's victory, for it seemed to carry fewer votes than ever, and Wallace did not carry Louisiana in the election.

Toward the end of the year, Perez appeared at Louisiana State University in Baton Rouge, his alma mater, to address the students. He made his usual claims of Communist infiltration of government, the need for states' rights and the worth of George Wallace. But he was heckled by the students, and refused to answer questions after his address. As he stormed out of the auditorium, the audience chanted, "There goes the Judge." The following day, the student newspaper the *Daily Reveille* commented that students "will not accept his 'simple' explanations like their parents have."

Perez retreated to Plaquemines to lick his wounds. He went duck hunting at the camp at Tiger Pass in January with friends, and one morning after dressing for the hunt complained that he wasn't feeling well. All but two of the other hunters went out without him; within a few minutes Perez suffered a heart attack. The two men rushed him north to Venice, after radioing the parish police, and Perez was given oxygen before being taken to the General Hospital in Port Sulphur, where police and parish officials had gathered.

The Judge responded well to treatment. After a few days, he was flown by helicopter to the Baptist Hospital in New Orleans, where his condition continued to improve. He was switched from intensive care to a private room, which overflowed with flowers from well-wishers. He spent four weeks in the hospital, carrying on business by telephone and by calling family and associates into his room. Doctors were optimistic about his prospects for recovery.

Perez was transferred to his ranch at Idlewild, where he continued to improve. He conducted private and some parish affairs from his office there. On the night of March 19, while talking to an associate and, according to observers, in good spirits, he suffered another heart attack and died with the telephone receiver in his hand. He was seventy-seven.

The Plaquemines *Gazette* described the scene as follows: "He was alone in his study when he breathed his last, when his stout heart stopped, causing him to topple from a chair where he was found within a few short minutes by his late wife's sister. . . . Like his beloved wife, Judge Perez had been told that day by his doctor that he could plan resuming his activities in moderation. He had even stopped off at his New Orleans office. Returning to Idlewild, he enjoyed his dinner—and then it happened. . . . Word of his death shocked his relatives, friends and associates and the countless thousands who looked upon Judge Perez as their protector, their friend."

The announcement of Judge Perez's death in the *Gazette* included a statement of the Perez family's wish that mourners would send money instead of flowers, to help finance Plaquemines's private school system. "In compliance with this request, and because of the pride Judge Perez felt in the development of the private schools of the Parish, which gives parents a choice for their children," the *Gazette* offered to publish the names of donors.

Perez's body was displayed the next day in the House of Bultman funeral home in New Orleans, where many mourners filed past the silver casket. Congressman Hébert, unable to leave the hospital after an eye operation, wrote an open letter to the family and the people of Plaquemines in which he said, "another great American now belongs to the ages. For over 30 years Judge Perez has been my political and personal friend. . . . He was a man in whom there was unlimited determination and a fiery tenacity for the things in which he believed. He asked no quarter and gave no quarter. Even those who did not understand him were compelled to respect him. . . . There were those who fought him but there were none who did not respect the valor of his shield. . . . Not only I, but everyone, friend and foe, will miss him. As I so often said in his lifetime and again say on his death, he was the 'noblest Roman of them all.' "

The *Gazette* reported that thousands of mourners visited the funeral home, and that they were "eloquent in their manifestations of grief, love, devotion and admiration for a man whom they believed to be a true friend, a leader of vision and compassion, a noble statesman, an astute lawyer, a defender of the people's rights and one of the greatest American patriots this country has known, a man who had the courage and ability to dissent when principles and his convictions were in jeopardy." The paper added that Perez was "not only the leader but the father of the parish."

The question being asked in Plaquemines and throughout Louisiana was how Perez's funeral would be conducted. His excommunication seemed to preclude a Catholic service, and there was general surprise, and amazement on the part of priests within the archdiocese, when the family announced that a Mass would be conducted at the same church where Mama Perez's funeral had been held, the Holy Name of Jesus Church on the Loyola University campus in uptown New Orleans, one of the most prestigious churches in the city.

On the morning of March 21, the Judge's family and close friends gathered at the funeral home on St. Charles Avenue for brief ceremonies. A group of children from the Prytania Private School entered the home in procession, carrying a heart-shaped arrangement of red and white carnations. A short prayer was said, and the coffin was closed and covered with roses. More than two hundred cars joined the procession uptown to Loyola. Motorcycle policemen from St. Bernard led the way, followed by New Orleans motorcycle policemen and members of the state police. Cars were parked for blocks up and down St. Charles from the church; several cab drivers delivered their fares, then parked their cabs and joined the crowd that overflowed the church and blocked the pavement. Among the dignitaries present were Governor Williams of Mississippi; Senator Eastland; Louisiana's lieutenant governor, Taddy Aycock; Associate Justice Tom Brady of Mississippi; scores of state representatives and senators, and practically every public official of Plaquemines and St. Bernard parishes.

George Wallace also attended, accompanied by a contingent of Perez admirers from Alabama. Wallace and George Singelmann embraced, both of them weeping.

The casket was rolled up the church steps, where Perez's seven grandsons lifted it and carried it inside, placing it near the altar. Three burning candles were placed on each side of the casket, and a crucifix stood behind it. The service was conducted by the Reverend Peter Boerding of St. Thomas Church in Pointe a la Hache, and the Reverend Stanley Goote, the latest head of Our Lady of Perpetual Help Church in Belle Chasse. Boerding began the mass by saying, "We humbly pray You . . . do not hand him over to the powers of evil, but command his soul to be taken up by the Holy Angels." Goote intoned, "Hear us, oh Lord. . . . Answer our prayers for Leander."

After communion, the church bells began to toll, and the casket was carried out. Mourners jammed the pavement and the lawn, where Wallace told newsmen, "I loved the Judge personally," and added, with little originality, "He was the noblest Roman of them all." The casket was then driven down into Plaquemines, a scene described by the *Gazette*: "The long procession of cars wound its way across the . . . bridge. . . . The business places closed and people lined the highway to pay their respects as this 'once in a century man' made his last trip. It was a beautiful day. The sun came out from behind the morning clouds as if to throw light on this man's soul as his casket was carried by his seven grandsons . . . blanketed with red roses along the stone path that leads to the chapel at the rear of the ranch home. The flowers were bursting with fullness. The moss from the giant Oak trees tossed in the gentle breeze. The birds sang like in a Requiem in his honor. Otherwise there was silence, a dignity befitting this great man. The mourners stood numb as the last ritual was performed by the priests attended by altar boys. Then the scraping of the coffin being put into the crypt, cut into the hearts of those who stood by helplessly. The rose blanket was placed in front of the crypt and the entourage passed through the Chapel to see where their loved one and friend was lain."

Father Boerding sprinkled holy water on the casket, and said, "God has taken him to Himself from the trials of this world." He asked that God not punish Perez for his sins but "make him a companion of Your saints."

"It was the end," reported the *Gazette*. "The end of a full and fruitful life, so well acknowledged that governors, statesmen, judges and other dignitaries and people from various walks of life, came from other parts of the country to pay their last respects."

In a telegram to the Perez family, Senator Russell Long said, "It was with deep regret that I learned of the tragic loss of your father. . . . It has been said that some people never stand for anything. That cannot be said of your father, who was an indefatigable fighter for his convictions. His dedication to the Bill of Rights, the causes of Home Rule and States' Rights, have already erected a monument to him in the hearts of many Americans."

Governor McKeithen, who attended the final ceremonies at the Idlewild mausoleum, declared that he had lost "a personal and dear friend . . . a strong man, a leader and a fighter in causes he thought were right."

George Wallace lamented the "loss to his state, the Southland and to the entire nation. [Perez] served his people well in many positions of leadership and will long be remembered for the contributions he made to the welfare of all of the people of his state and nation."

Former governor Jimmie Davis said, "There are many who might have disagreed with the causes he championed, but there are few who would disagree with the personal sincerity and integrity of Judge Perez himself. He did what he . . . believed was right. And this is as much as any man can do in his lifetime."

Another former governor of Louisiana, Robert Kennon, confessed that he found Perez "really Louisiana's most interesting political figure. Over the years he has been much loved by those who knew him well. His death is the passing of an era in Louisiana history."

Even the New Orleans *Times-Picayune*, for years a critic of Perez and Plaquemines politics, waxed sentimental: "A half-century career as a strong warrior for and against causes and political figures came to an end with the death of Leander Henry Perez, Sr. . . . Despite his harshness, with no holds barred in his public battles, he was pleasant and attractive in his private relationships. He was a resourceful lawyer and an able champion of what he chose to advocate. . . . Judge Perez made a lasting mark on Louisiana political life and his death leaves a hollow in the public affairs of his parish that will not be filled as it was during his lifetime."

In Plaquemines Parish, on the night of Perez's death, five young black men entered a bar owned by a white man. They bought whiskey, and said they intended to celebrate. Shortly thereafter, sheriff's deputies arrived and arrested the men for "disturbing the peace." They were handcuffed and transported across the river to Pointe a la Hache, where they were finger-printed, photographed, and then released on bond. All five defendants showed up for trial, expecting to be found not guilty or to pay only small fines; instead, they were convicted and sentenced to jail.

Loyal Opposition

The Plaquemines Parish Commission Council met after Perez's funeral, beginning with a one-minute silent prayer for the late Judge. It was unanimously decreed that "the birthdate of Plaquemines's Great Father," July 16, be an official parish holiday. The resolution was introduced by Luke Petrovich, who called Perez "one of our greatest assets—a natural resource, so to speak." It was also unanimously decreed that in honor of "the dear departed father of Plaquemines Parish . . . brilliant statesman, noble leader, and truly Great American," and due to his "love, devotion and untiring efforts"—especially his "Herculean" efforts in rebuilding the parish after hurricane Betsy—all flags in the parish would fly at half-mast for two weeks.

One week after the funeral Mass, six New Orleans priests lodged a complaint with Archbishop Philip Hannan, protesting the burial of "the leading racist of the South, Leander H. Perez, Sr., with full and solemn honors in a Catholic church." An unidentified official of the archdiocese announced to the Associated Press that the excommunication of Judge Perez had in fact been quietly lifted the previous year. Officials of the archdiocese had begun discreet inquiries after the death of Mama Perez in 1967 to determine whether Judge Perez wished to return officially to the Catholic faith. Archbishop Rummel, who had initiated the excommunication, had died in the interim. Perez was made to understand that anything he might say in public that could be construed as "supporting the authority of the Church" would be sufficient to lift the censure. It was claimed that one year before his death, Perez spoke to a small gathering which included two priests, at the dedication of an incinerator plant in Plaquemines. They reported to their superiors that Perez had ended his brief speech with a word of praise for the parochial school system, and for the new archbishop, Hannan. Soon after that, Perez was informed that he was absolved.

Little more than a month after Perez's death, his son Lea, the district attorney, traveled with some deputies up to New Orleans and attempted to make an arrest—both out of their legal parish jurisdiction and within the confines of the federal court building. Lawrence Rousselle and his lawyer, Ben Smith, had been scheduled to appear in Plaquemines's court that same day for trial on the dubious aggravated-assault charge against Rousselle, and had come to federal court in an attempt to have the case transferred, claiming that Rousselle could not get a fair trial in Plaquemines. Rousselle, his wife Shirley, and Smith were standing in the hallway outside a federal courtroom when Lea and his men appeared; they grabbed Rousselle, who was dissuaded by his wife from resisting, and Smith, and attempted to drag them from the building. Smith broke away and pounded on the door of the courtroom, and only the intervention of a federal judge prevented them from being taken back down to Plaquemines for trial.

Those in power in Plaquemines are much less inclined to arrest Rousselle on trumped-up charges because he is represented by an able lawyer, and because he doesn't hesitate to file his own charges against those who violate his rights. "The first time I went into that courtroom," Rousselle remembers, "they treated me like crap. Now when I show up at Pointe a la Hache, the judge says, 'Get Mr. Rousselle a chair.' "

Rousselle decided to run for office for the first time in the local elections of November 1971. The Independents changed their name to the Plaquemines Parish Loyal Democrats, aligning themselves with the loyalist and progressive faction now dominating Louisiana politics; Rousselle announced his candidacy for the office of clerk of court, and another loyalist, Punt Sisung, ran for sheriff. Sisung (he pronounces his name "Caesar") is an ex-deputy for the Plaquemines sheriff's office who backed the wrong candidate ten years ago and was dismissed on charges of brutality. He owned the Party Tavern in Venice, not far from the Jump at the bottom of the parish, in the shadow of the cracking plants where crude oil is processed and the tank farms where it is stored. Sisung owns property in the area, and is considered a local patriarch. He was sent down by the sheriff to clean up the Jump in the early 1940's, when lower Plaquemines was truly a wilderness and even the fittest sometimes didn't survive. "Ex-cons drifted down here from every part of the country to work the oil rigs," Sisung says. "People got murdered all kinds of ways. They sent me down here because they needed a *man*. I got shot three times" (he pauses to touch various parts of his large body) "but I managed to put the stick on that trash, and I beat them to pieces."

Sisung still wears his old deputy's trousers with a dark stripe down the side, which he tucks into the tops of his work boots; he doesn't smoke or drink, and prefers to talk politics out in front of his tavern, away from the fishermen pulling on cans of Dixie beer.

"Judge Perez was Hitler the Second," Sisung said, after announcing his candidacy. "He ruined this parish politically, made millions in oil and sulphur. His sons—the royalty—are doing the same thing. I'm running for sheriff, and I plan to win. When I do win, I'll take a spade handle to the foot of those courthouse steps, and the pimps and the royalty's puppets will be jumping out the windows."

Sisung was widely known in the parish, particularly in the lower half, the traditional seat of anti-Perez sentiment. He owned several businesses in the area of Venice, and provided jobs and general advice. During the hurricanes, Sisung was usually the last man to leave the area, and during Camille he had to tie himself, a woman, and a child to a telephone pole and remain there through the night until the storm had passed. Both he and Rousselle believed they had a chance to win the election. They were encouraged by what they took to be signs of changing times and erosion of the Perezes' power. The candidate backed by the family in the recent election for a seat on the court of appeals had lost; some parish employees told them in private that they would vote for them. State politics had in general been radically changed when the United States District Court reapportioned the legislature (after the legislators themselves had failed to do so), reducing the total number of legislative seats and greatly increasing urban and black representation.

Sisung drove up the highway from Venice before the election, ringing doorbells and handing out his meager campaign literature. Rousselle fitted his Volkswagen with loudspeakers and drove down the road from Belle Chasse, talking to the people about the need for good local government and enough jobs. At one point during their campaign, Sisung said, "The royalty can kill me, but they can't scare me."

Rousselle, realistic and determined, said, "The antis have gotten almost a third of the vote cast in every election since 1959. People used to tell me I was crazy to oppose the Perez family. Now they're telling me they hope we'll win. The 18-year-old vote will help, because the kids in this parish hate the Perezes. Every time I see a kid hitchhiking, I pick him up, and we start talking."

Rousselle and Sisung were backed by the habitual antis, including the veteran opposition candidate Ernest Hingle, who had fled Plaquemines to become an expatriate farmer up in Picayune, Mississippi. Hingle claimed that he would write a book about Judge Perez and Plaquemines Parish that would reveal a half-century of corruption there and throughout Louisiana, and although he has not produced the book, he continues to offer advice and support to the loyalists.

The courthouse crowd was forced to exert itself in the campaign as it hadn't in years. Perez candidates gave free ice cream to children all over the parish and held many political rallies; checks for hurricane relief were given out from funds that had been mysteriously unavailable until then. One observer said, "Those white boys from the courthouse even had to go into black people's homes and sit down and drink a black man's coffee."

Shortly before the election, the incumbent faction, including a member of the Commission Council, paraded down Highway 23 on the west bank of the river through Belle Chasse. When they passed the building owned by Rousselle, where he had once operated his laundry, they pasted one of their posters on the store front. Rousselle's sixteen-year-old son attempted to stop them, and was squirted in the face with Mace. He went home and got his father, who drove him to a local drive-in, hoping that he could identify his assailant. Several of the paraders dragged Rousselle from his car. According to Rousselle, he hit one man between the eyes "and he started shaking like a big ole hog. He almost went down, but he grabbed me by the arm, and I gave him a couple more punches under the heart. Another man tried to squirt Mace in my eyes, but I saw it coming and closed them. Then I ran."

Rousselle managed to get away unhurt. His assailants vented their wrath on Rousselle's car, and destroyed his loudspeakers. Rousselle later filed suit in federal court against the Commission Council member.

The election was held, and Rousselle and Sisung lost by more than two-thirds of the vote. Several people complained that they had difficulty in manipulating the levers for loyalist candidates in the voting machines. The loyalists had asked for federal observers, but the Justice Department did not supply them. Afterwards, Rousselle said bitterly, "If we had black candidates, we would have gotten federal observers." They might also have been helped by coverage in the Plaquemines *Gazette*—to this day still a Perez house organ that doesn't necessarily even print the names of opposition candidates on its mock ballots.

Rousselle claimed not to be discouraged. The district attorney's race was coming up in August 1972, and he began to look around for a good candidate to back against Lea Perez. The race included all of the Twenty-fifth Judicial District; since St. Bernard's population today is more than fifty thousand—twice that of Plaquemines—it made sense to find a candidate from St. Bernard. A young lawyer named Emanuel Fernandez and a resident of St. Bernard announced he would run as a "reform" candidate, and within days two of his relatives working in the registrar's office were replaced by Kelly Girls.

Rousselle agreed to introduce Fernandez to the antis in Plaquemines. Such tours usually began at the bottom of the parish, and necessarily included the home of Punt Sisung—now a trailer, since all of his houses had been washed away in the last storm. Sisung received Rousselle, Fernandez, and Fernandez's manager cordially, still wearing his old deputy's trousers, but during the discussion of the upcoming election lay back in his reclining chair, seeming distracted and uncommunicative. Fernandez outlined his reform plans, based on the appeal of being a "full-time district attorney" who would provide faster, more thorough investigation, would prosecute his own cases and reduce favoritism.

As the men were leaving, Sisung told them, "I wish you boys luck, but I'm through with politics. Them people at the courthouse hurt me bad. I can't get my insurance money, can't get a loan. Yes sir, I'm through with politics."

Rousselle drove on up the highway, followed by Fernandez and his manager, and he said without rancor, "I don't know how they did it, but they [the courthouse clique] managed to get to Punt."

Rousselle and other loyalists backed Fernandez because he was the only candidate with a chance of defeating Lea Perez. Fernandez lost the election.

Rousselle refuses to lose hope. In the Louisiana elections, candidates for both governor and lieutenant-governor backed by the Perezes were defeated. The new governor, a liberal named Edwin Edwards, is one of the few southern Louisiana Catholics ever elected to the post; he waged a sophisticated television campaign and proved that the conservative upstate vote—which Judge Perez had always counted on—was no longer necessary to win a statewide election. Antis in general see signs that the Perez power is declining in the fact that Lea and Chalin Perez are not often seen in the parish, and that their influence on a state level is minimal (Chalin failed to gain control of a committee studying prospective sites for a superport to be built in the Gulf). But the number of patronage jobs in Plaquemines is greater than ever and the loyalists who backed Edwards in the run-off election hoped to get some concessions from the new and supposedly sympathetic governor, including an end to parish maintenance of state roads in Plaquemines, which provided even more patronage jobs.

Lawrence Rousselle was one of forty-five insurgents who attended the Plaquemines Democratic caucus in April 1972, convened to choose delegates to the upcoming Democratic National Convention. These antis joined almost one thousand Perez followers outside the courthouse at Pointe a la Hache, and their slate included young people, blacks, and women who leaned toward George McGovern. The insurgents were treated politely, although Commission Council member Luke Petrovich, the number-three man in the parish, called Rousselle a liar when Rousselle told a reporter that the political system in Plaquemines is still "run on control."

Most of the Perez followers at the caucus held parish jobs, or were related to those who did. One employee confessed secretly, "My boss told me, 'If you value your job, be down here today.'"

Rousselle and other insurgents were allowed time to speak to the gathering. Such blatant opposition during Judge Perez's reign, as *The New York Times* commented, "would have been almost unthinkable."

Lea Perez's men handed out bologna and cheese sandwiches to the crowd; the occasion differed considerably from the old days featuring brass bands and little balls, but none of the insurgent delegates were elected. Those who were elected (all white and including only one woman) were technically uncommitted, but were known to support George Wallace.

"You know where we were four years ago," Chalin Perez told the crowd. "And that's where we'll be this coming election."

Petrovich later said, "The national situation is worse than it was in 1968. What do the Democrats have to offer us? Their front-runner is McGovern. My God! An absolute collectivist, a Socialist, anti-American. And next to him is Humphrey!"

Rousselle, along with the other antis, is accustomed to the name-calling and the rhetoric. His efforts to change things in Plaquemines have hurt him financially and placed a considerable emotional strain on him and his family. But he refuses to leave the parish or to quit opposition politics, in spite of the fact that it is often a lonely, uncomfortable, and discouraging avocation.

"I'm staying involved until the Perezes get voted out," Rousselle vows. "Petrovich once said that I've got my price, and he's right. My price is their jobs."

Heirs Apparent

There are no longer "Colored" and "White" signs on the restroom doors in the courthouse at Pointe a la Hache. In fact there are no signs at all, so that anyone unfamiliar with the building must ask directions of the secretaries, parish officials, or politicians—and they are still all white. Judge Leon still presides in the courtroom on the second floor, where windows overlook the levee and the river, and passing freighters seem close enough to touch. On a bright spring day, when heat simmers over the dun-colored water, and the voice of the assistant district attorney or of a parish prisoner in striped fatigues drones on about some minor offense, time and place seem irreconcilable: this rural scene belongs to another, simpler era, despite the contemporary humming of the air conditioner.

The district attorney's office on the same floor retains the atmosphere of privilege: lackadaisical good manners and total imperviousness. Several swarthy, resolute men in tropical suits lounge in the outer office, blocking access to Lea Perez, who may or may not be in the building; one of his men thumbs through a brochure put out by a manufacturer of automatic weapons.

Across the hall in the voter registrar's office, Roy Lyons chews on an unlit cigar that might have been unwrapped and placed between his teeth three decades before. He tells a stranger asking the number of registered voters in Plaquemines Parish, "I can't give that information to someone just walking in off the street," though he is required by law to do just that.

The clerk of court, Allen Lobrano, manages to suppress all but a flicker of a smile when he claims not to know the exact number of absentee ballots cast in the last election. (Allen Lobrano looks remarkably like his brother Robert, Judge Perez's close associate in early Plaquemines land dealing, though they are easily distinguished because Robert Lobrano has a plug missing from one ear in the exact shape of a set of human teeth.) Absentee ballots have long been in Plaquemines a means of controlling a considerable percentage of the vote, and they still are.

Downstairs, in the new courthouse wing, are located the offices of the members of the Commission Council and the small auditorium where they gather on the second Wednesday of every month to take up parish business. The oval table sits in the shadow of a six-hundred-pound marlin; every resident of Plaquemines knows the day the council meets, but the audience is likely to be limited to old Ben Meyer, once an archfoe of Judge Perez but in later years accepted into the fold and made the official "parish historian," and Burt Hyde, a gravel-voiced veteran reporter for the New Orleans *States-Item* and a friend of the late Judge, who still considers critics of the Perezes as lacking the sense "to pour piss out of a boot."

Sitting at the table with the council is Mrs. Joseph Sendker, editor of the *Gazette*, dressed as if for some special social event, dutifully recording the council's unanimous decisions, for there is still no other kind of decision in Plaquemines Parish. Chalin Perez—short, stout, and more obviously of Spanish descent than his father—presides with a dogged efficiency that seems to border upon boredom. He dresses stylishly—wide lapels, a striped tie, these innovations imitated by two other council members, Luke Petrovich and Howard Wilcox. But Clarence Kimble's rumpled seersucker and stringy tie seem to have endured since the middle years of the Judge's reign; he fingers the cuff of Chalin's mohair jacket at the conclusion of the meeting, and exclaims, "Don't he look *nice?*"

Neither Chalin nor his brother Lea is an easy man to catch when he comes down to the courthouse. Those rare days are spent delegating authority in meetings and impromptu conferences, and discussing problems with parish officials and those in the private school system. Outsiders are definitely in the way, a sentiment that extends beyond the courthouse. A visit to the low, prefabricated building housing the Promised Land Academy, situated behind the Judge's old raised plantation home a few miles upstream from Pointe a la Hache, and surrounded by yellow buses owned by the Commission Council, reveals a couple of hundred white students sitting silently at desks, in attitudes that can only be described as mock-studious. The Academy's principal will become irate at the knowledge that a stranger is in his halls, banish him "until I check with Chalin," and refuse even to let him take photographs.

On court days, Lea Perez can usually be found on the ferry during the 5:00 P.M. crossing to the west bank. Lea (known as "Mister Lee") is considered the more personable and approachable of the Perez brothers, an unpretentious man in spite of his patrician Southern accent ("tuhn" for "turn," "fo-uh" for "four"), a man who enjoys a good party and a good hunt. His home in Plaquemines is a kind of shrine built to his prowess as a hunter on African safaris, and the sitting room includes the remains of more than a dozen exotic animals (including a bull elephant and half a mandrill baboon). Lea will sit on the fender of his midnight blue Oldsmobile Delta Royale during the ferry crossing and talk, revealing nothing substantial about himself or his father except, inadvertently, the considerable difference between being a Perez in Plaquemines and being an average citizen. He is talking when the ferry docks, and the cars parked behind the Delta Royale go through intricate backing-up maneuvers to disembark without disturbing him.

Lea drives up Highway 23 toward Idlewild. Another Oldsmobile belonging to the district attorney's office is parked in the grass at the side of the road, and Lea pulls over and gets out to have a private conference with one of his investigators. He produces a package of local Picayune cigarettes, lights one, listens to the younger man's intense monologue. A third Oldsmobile appears on the horizon, sails through the high grass; a short, muscular man in a sport shirt steps out and joins the other two. As if by prearrangement, the men turn and walk ten paces toward the levee, leaving a cloud of bothersome gnats abandoned.

The conference is concluded as abruptly as it began. Lea continues up the highway to his expansive brick home, bumps across the cattle grate, and passes between rows of manicured orange trees. Before going into the house through a back door, he inspects the blooms and complains of starlings that pick at the buds, which later produce damaged fruit.

Inside, the house is neatly kept, and empty; Lea's wife and children are either at home in New Orleans or away at school. Within view of a stuffed water buffalo, he mixes Beefeaters gin and quinine water; he admits that he was "tapped" by his father to become district attorney. What seems to be a weariness with parish affairs and with the additional complications in St. Bernard—including the necessity of being re-elected by all those transplanted city constituents—might be due in part to an introspection not shared by his father or his brother. When Lea Perez says, "Daddy wanted the government of the parish to stay in the family. He worked very hard, and we work very hard, to make sure every dollar is spent wisely," the words have a too-familiar ring.

Next door to Lea's house is the old clapboard ranch house occupied by the Judge and Mama Perez before Perez had the columned brick home constructed on the far side among the massive oaks hung with Spanish moss. Behind it stands the mausoleum. No member of the Perez family lives in the big house; it is kept by a black man and woman, and supervised by Dutch Assavedo, Perez's old bodyguard, who lives nearby. Dutch takes time off from his duties as special investigator for Lea Perez to cut the grass around the place; he is still fiercely loyal to the memory of the Judge, to Lea and Chalin Perez, and he still believes in an ongoing "Zionist conspiracy" to take over America. In a closet in his own house, Dutch keeps a furled white flag trimmed in gold, which bears a red cross, the name "Christian Patriots," and the slogan, "God Is Our Creator."

"The people of America are not stupid," Dutch says with controlled rage. "They know what the Communists and the Jews are up to. The good Christians of this country are just laying low and waiting. In a few years you're going to see this flag flying all over America. When I say the Apostles' Creed, I say God is my creator into the white race, and I'm proud."

Assavedo considers Judge Perez "so great a man that you can hardly describe him. He was a great Christian patriot. I really didn't think the Judge would die so soon—I thought the Lord would keep him here a while longer to help the American people."

Dutch is the man credited by members of the Plaquemines DA's office with wielding a machine gun while on official parish business with the Judge. Asked about this, Dutch is quick to make the point that "fully automatic guns are against the law in this country." Then he opens the trunk of his Oldsmobile, parked in the driveway of the Judge's home, revealing an array of weapons including long clubs, two shotguns, several hatchets, a Bowie knife, and a blunt heavy weapon that certainly appears to be a machine gun. He takes this gun out, clutches the stock close to his sturdy body, and pumps half-a-dozen slugs into the ground at the foot of an oak, throwing clods of dirt high into the air, shattering momentarily the rural Delta calm, and mixing smells of burnt cordite and orange blossoms.

"Did you see me pull the trigger each time?" Dutch asks. "This is a *semi*-automatic machine gun."

Chalin Perez's official Plaquemines residence is at Stella, a hamlet on the east bank of the river, which qualifies him to run for the pivotal position of Commissioner of Public Affairs, the Judge's old office. Chalin is more likely to be found in the suite of law offices of Leander Perez and Sons on the top floor of the Commerce Building in New Orleans, where Delta Development is also located. George Singelmann, balding and plump, also hangs out at the Perez law office when he isn't busy at the Citizens Council headquarters trying to raise membership. Singelmann organized a large collection of Perez's personal papers, "a whole world of stuff," according to Singelmann, that was burned on the Judge's orders before his death.

Although Chalin has black hair and doesn't habitually wear glasses, he has inherited his father's imperious reticence, his ploy of raising his chin and regarding his questioner from beneath half-closed eyelids, and the cigar. He is cool, decisive, slightly deprecating, and respectable; his view of world affairs, like his father's, tends to be simplistic, if apologetic.

"The Judge never said that everyone involved in civil rights was a Communist. He said they were influenced by Communists. He was always against subversive groups, he knew they were behind integration activities. Part of the Communist Manifesto says they want to create a black nation. If my father was here, he'd tell you what to read to prove it. . . . Two of the Communist countries put us on their mailing lists, and their literature said they were counting on the Fair Employment Practices Commission to create hate between the races.

"My father never said that Negroes were inferior. He said that integration in schools wouldn't work, and it hasn't. The people in our area are the only ones in the country who still have freedom of choice in selecting schools. The private schools in Plaquemines have helped the public ones because there are no animosities—the kids know they're there because their parents want it."

Chalin doesn't foresee any change in the make-up of government in Plaquemines. "Why shouldn't we be re-elected?" he asks. "I serve in Plaquemines because it's my duty. . . . My father remained in office for so long because he was dedicated to the people. Nothing he ever did was illegal, immoral, or incorrect."

Many people in Plaquemines say that Chalin rules as the sequestered chairman of the board and major stockholder, instead of as the histrionic leader embodying the traits of his people, as Perez's supporters claimed of the Judge. Walter Blaize, the sheriff installed by the state Guard, who stayed active in Plaquemines politics until his recent death, once said, "The sons are worse than the father. At least you could talk to the old man."

The sons may have inherited their father's beliefs, but they lack his sense of mission. The Perez family contributed the largest single bundle to George Wallace's 1972 presidential campaign—twenty thousand dollars—and Chalin says he would like "to turn this country around," but neither he nor Lea offers active right-wing leadership in the South. At home in Plaquemines, dominance by one man and one idea is no longer so grossly obvious. Father Gootee, still pastor of Our Lady of Perpetual Help in Belle Chasse, says, "The feeling of dictatorship has passed." But the machine and the power remain.

Chalin's son, Chalin O. Perez, Jr., graduated from Tulane University with a degree in economics in 1972, and entered law school there, like his father and his grandfather before him. Chalin Junior's nickname among friends and fraternity brothers is "Cop"—his initials. He is a sports fan and an ardent outdoorsman; the walls of his apartment in uptown New Orleans are decorated with enlarged color posters of hanging mallard ducks and freshly caught trout. Like his father and grandfather, Cop Perez is short and stocky, but fair-complected, with an open, extrovert's expression and traditional Southern manners. On most Saturday mornings he is up early, in front of the portable television set transmitting from the center of his coffee table, preparing for a hunting or fishing trip with school friends down in Plaquemines.

Cop was one of several grandsons bearing the Judge's casket down the church steps in 1969. He remembers his grandfather fondly as a man "who liked to have fun, and didn't give advice. He just told me hunting stories, and taught me how to shoot animals. He was so much more than a big power politician. He loved his people, and they inspired him. Those people down there are individuals. They lead a good life—they work for a living, and they have fun."

Before attending Tulane, Cop went to various Catholic prep schools, including Canterbury in New Milford, Connecticut. "There were no freaks up there then," he says. "Now it's ninety per cent dope." He made good grades, though he was primarily interested in sports. Although described by acquaintances as "super rich" and "super Catholic," Cop is a firm exponent of the Protestant ethic: "I was raised to believe that you have to prove yourself. You have to earn everything you get. I've been raised strictly, without a big allowance. I just go to my father and tell him what I need to live on. I'm perfectly happy—I don't believe in spoiling people. . . . I have a better social background than ninety per cent of the whites in this country. I believe that you have to have a lower class, or else there's trouble. A kid of somebody working in a factory or somewhere like that might think they should be equal—have what I have—and they might go out and just steal what they want."

The origin of the Perez fortune, estimated as high as one hundred million, doesn't concern Cop. He believes his grandfather "made his money during the oil boom. He was on top of the situation, I imagine he bought land with oil on it." He also dismisses charges that Judge Perez was senile toward the end of his life, and that he was a racist: "Everybody's some kind of a racist. Look what's happening up north right now, with the opposition to busing. I was disappointed when there was no resistance to busing down South. Integration of public schools is all right, but busing is ridiculous. . . . One trouble is that ninety per cent of the white people in this country don't have the emotional or intellectual ability to understand why they shouldn't go out with colored people."

Asked about the high rate of unemployment among blacks in Plaquemines, he says, "The blacks contribute nothing to the parish. Ninety per cent of them are on welfare. Why not give the jobs to the whites, who are productive? The coloreds just sit around and live off everybody else. I believe in survival of the fittest, like back in the pioneer days. I've worked with blacks down there on the ranch—they have no motivation or pride in themselves. It's impossible for them to reach a state of equality. . . . Why shove a black up the ladder instead of a white?"

Cop Perez believes that leadership is a rare and ineffable quality, and noblesse oblige an enduring reality: "There's no way to have real equality. Even on *Star Trek* on television, everybody's supposed to be equal, but you know that Captain

Kirk is the leader, because every decision he makes is perfect. . . . Louisiana has changed a lot since my grandfather's time: it's more complicated now. When he became head of Plaquemines, there was only one road and two levees, and the big thing for him was building locks for the fishermen. Now my father is planning a four-lane highway to Venice, three marinas and an airport. . . . It certainly isn't an easy life, even though you get public recognition. My father didn't really have a choice."

Cop knows no people his own age in Plaquemines, just friends of his father and his uncle, and those left over from the days of the Judge. He is well acquainted with the procedure and the efficacy of entertaining legislators and businessmen in the hunting and fishing camps at the Mississippi's mouth, the tradition of public affairs conducted in obscurity—that effortless meshing of business and politics. This is the way it has always been; this is necessary.

Cop Perez is his grandfather's triumph, and not only because he shares the old man's racial myopia. Judge Perez never did a thing without calculation, and his obsession with power and his complacency grew out of rampant ego and a knowledge of human venality, rather than from any illusions of intrinsic worth. His own son inherited that complacency; Chalin Perez also inherited his father's cynicism. When Chalin speaks of responsibility and good government, he seems barely able to suppress a smirk—hardly an accouterment of the receptacle of the divine right to rule.

Cop Perez, however, is guileless and apparently unshakeable in his view of order, at least one aspect of what real nobility once called breeding. There is simply no question of right, for that is given. There is only one view, and that is proprietary. Cop claims to be "off and on" in his decision about whether or not to take over the responsibilities of government in Plaquemines, but he adds, "I will do anything I can to help those people down there."

A Note on the Author

James Conaway was born in Memphis, Tennessee, in 1941. He was graduated from Southwestern University in Memphis, and was a Wallace Stegner Fellow in Creative Writing at Stanford. From 1965 to 1967, Mr. Conaway was a reporter for the New Orleans *Times Picayune*, and he has since become a widely published free-lance writer whose work has appeared in *The Atlantic, The New York Times Magazine*, and other periodicals. He is also the author of a novel, *The Big Easy*, published in 1970.

A Note on the Type

This book was set in Caledonia, a Linotype face designed by W. A. Dwiggins. It belongs to the family of printing types called "modern face" by printers—a term used to mark the change in style of type letters that occurred about 1800. Caledonia borders on the general design of Scotch Modern, but is more freely drawn than that letter.

The book was composed by Pennset, Inc., Blooms-burg, Pennsylvania. It was printed and bound by The Colonial Press, Clinton, Mass. Typography and binding design by Carole Lowenstein.